Marmalade

SOCK MONKEY DREAMS

SOCK MONKEY DREAMS

daily life at the red heel monkey shelter

WHITNEY SHROYER & LETITIA WALKER

PHOTOGRAPHY BY MICHAEL TRAISTER

VIKING STUDIO

VIKING STUDIO
Published by the Penguin Group
Penguin Group (USA) Inc., 375 Hudson Street,
New York, New York 10014, U.S.A.
Penguin Group (Canada), 90 Eglinton Avenue East, Suite 700,
Toronto, Ontario, Canada M4P 2Y3
(a division of Pearson Penguin Canada Inc.)
Penguin Books Ltd, 80 Strand, London WC2R 0RL, England
Penguin Ireland, 25 St. Stephen's Green, Dublin 2, Ireland
(a division of Penguin Books Ltd)
Penguin Books Australia Ltd, 250 Camberwell Road, Camberwell,
Victoria 3124, Australia
(a division of Pearson Australia Group Pty Ltd)
Penguin Books India Pvt Ltd, 11 Community Centre, Panchsheel Park,
New Delhi – 110 017, India
Penguin Group (NZ), Cnr Airborne and Rosedale Roads, Albany,
Auckland 1310, New Zealand
(a division of Pearson New Zealand Ltd)
Penguin Books (South Africa) (Pty) Ltd, 24 Sturdee Avenue,
Rosebank, Johannesburg 2196, South Africa

Penguin Books Ltd, Registered Offices:
80 Strand, London WC2R 0RL, England

First published in 2006 by Viking Studio,
a member of Penguin Group (USA) Inc.

1 3 5 7 9 10 8 6 4 2

Copyright © Whitney Shroyer, Letitia Walker, and Michael Traister, 2006
All rights reserved

ISBN 0-670-03808-3

Printed in China
Set in Zurich BT
Designed by Jill Weber / Frajil Farms Productions

FOR MAGENTA AND DYLAN

"You should dream more . . .
Reality in our century is not
something to be faced."

—GRAHAM GREENE

THE RED HEEL MONKEY SHELTER

THE ORIGIN OF OUR SPECIES

BY FOLIO

Greetings, my dear friends! It is my pleasure to give some introductory remarks to this collection of observations and anecdotes about the Red Heel Monkey Shelter. When my colleague and longtime "Redheel,"* Benny Hathaway, asked if I would contribute a brief history of sock monkeys to his book, I was honored. Mr. Hathaway and his fellow Redheels are a beacon of aspiration for our curious little species (we belong to the genus *Sockosimian*). In creating and sustaining their community, the citizens of the Red Heel Monkey Shelter are pushing the social evolution of the sock monkey to its next logical step. It is with great pride that I number many of them my friends.

My name is Folio. I am a very old sock monkey. Time and circumstances have shriveled me to the point where I am roughly the size of a dried apricot. For some time now, I have whiled away my hours in a secondhand bookstore in a large college community not far from the Red Heel. I spend my days behind the counter† and my nights wandering among the stacks, educating myself on the subjects available to me in this revolving library I call home. I have spent many evenings among forgotten fabulists and fictioneers, historians and philosophers no longer taught or credited, and artists whose works have been boarded up in forgotten wings of museums. On my nightly explorations (I require no sleep nor rest, really, since flesh and blood are not mine to decry), I have paid special attention to any books that might provide a clue or some insight into the origin of my species.

That the history of the sock monkey is of particular interest to me should come as little shock to you, dear reader, for is not the bulk of your printed material an inquiry into human understanding? Few books have been published by or about sock monkeys, but most of these have crossed my paws at one time or another. I can therefore state with confidence that never before has so

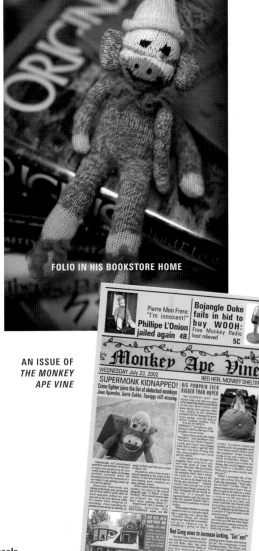

FOLIO IN HIS BOOKSTORE HOME

AN ISSUE OF
*THE MONKEY
APE VINE*

---

*Residents of the Red Heel Monkey Shelter refer to themselves as Redheels.
†I'm not working behind the counter. I'm more of what you might call décor or ambience.

much data about sock monkeys been compiled in one place by one of our own kind, let alone a monkey of some literary ability, as in *Sock Monkey Dreams.* Hathaway has the unique insights of a participant, the trained eye of an observer, the neutral voice of a reporter, the radical thought processes of a true reformer, and the dry wit of a born writer. He is far too modest to admit to many of these roles within the course of the pages of this book, or in his newspaper, *The Monkey Ape Vine,* so please allow me to do it for him.

I originally came upon a discarded copy of *The Monkey Ape Vine* in a derelict box of old comic books and other useless literary detritus. I was rather shocked to discover a newspaper written by a sock monkey for other sock monkeys, more so that it seemed to cover the doings of a dwelling known as the Red Heel Monkey Shelter. I pored over this paper, fascinated by the implications. I tracked down and contacted Mr. Hathaway. He was amazed that I knew of his paper and was even more surprised that I was interested in reading more ("It's just about a bunch of stuff that happens here. I never figured anyone else would care," said Hathaway). I requested a subscription to his periodical, and ever since have become more and more fond of the populace of the Red Heel Monkey Shelter and the little world they have created.

Sock dolls and their rather more dim-witted cousins, sock puppets, have been part of the American craftscape for as long as there have been toy creatures. When the Nelson Knitting Company of Rockford, Illinois, standardized and began distributing the pattern for the red heel sock monkey in 1954, the sock monkey rose to the forefront of domestically designed craft creatures. It is difficult for a toy creature with scant exposure to the mass media or mass production to retain popularity over the course of decades. That the

FO[I]IO FUN FACT

I feel one thing should be stated directly and immediately: We are not sock puppets. Sock puppets are a hose of an entirely different color, and it is not only incorrect but is considered taboo to refer to a sock monkey as a "sock puppet." Puppets are hollow and are manufactured to serve the needs and the words of another being. They are like parasites, attaching themselves onto the hand of a host in order to spring into personal existence. We, however, are complete in and of ourselves—solid, three-dimensional beings who do not collapse into undefined flatness because of the lack of a host. It is a strangely common perception to assume that all creatures derived from socks are sock puppets, and I strongly hope this book puts that particular notion to rest once and for all.

THE EVOLUTION OF

AMOEBABY
FIFI

NEANDERDOLL
ARTURO

sock monkey has accomplished this for more than fifty years is a testament to its resonance, looks, and charm, three factors essential to craft creature reproduction.

During the Depression, store-bought toys were desirable but unattainable extravagances, especially in rural Middle America. And while such folk forms as the corn-husk doll or the bottlecap baby were popular distractions, both lacked a certain snugglesome comfort that children crave. Thrifty mothers, accustomed to using a piece of material over and over, refashioned worn work socks into primitive creatures that they stuffed with leftover rags and other castoffs.

These "neanderdolls" were the predecessors of the sock monkey. They were only half formed, mainly because each was made with only one sock! Just as human beings need two sets of chromosomes, a sock monkey needs a left and right sock to take on its proper form. Neanderdoll construction varied widely and chaotically from creator to creator; clearly something was missing that was necessary for the sock creature to achieve craftical mass. That missing element turned out to be the red heel. John Nelson patented his sock loom in 1880. Nelson Knitting was not the first company to mass-produce socks, but it was the first to manufacture them without a seam in the toe or heel. Seams in the heel are uncomfortable to the backs of people's feet, so the Nelson socks became very popular. So popular, in fact, that a number of companies began producing similar socks with the well-known brown and cream pattern design, a style of socks called Rockfords. In 1932, Nelson Knitting began using a circular red heel design on their socks and called them Original Rockfords. When Nelson Knitting created the red heel, the company became the unknowing forefather of our species. Finally, the perfect material for a cute, cheerful companion for children was found.

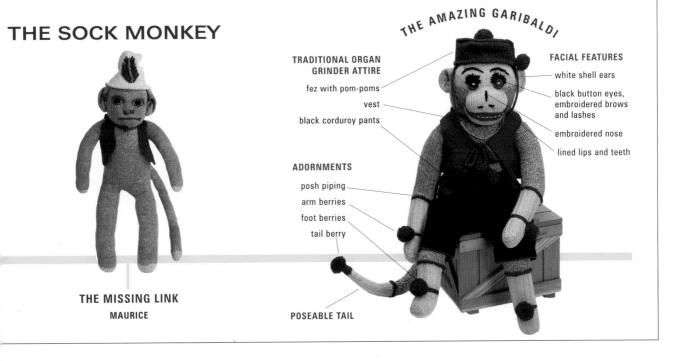

THE SOCK MONKEY

THE MISSING LINK
MAURICE

THE AMAZING GARIBALDI

TRADITIONAL ORGAN GRINDER ATTIRE
fez with pom-poms
vest
black corduroy pants

ADORNMENTS
posh piping
arm berries
foot berries
tail berry

POSEABLE TAIL

FACIAL FEATURES
white shell ears
black button eyes, embroidered brows and lashes
embroidered nose
lined lips and teeth

The red heel gives the monkey a great deal of its personality and character. Two heels, one for the mouth and one for the behind, give shape and symmetry to the sock monkey. Early sock creatures lacked this built-in mouth (and the embarrassing but amusing posterior), and neanderdolls' stitched lines lacked the wide-open friendly grin of the red heel. I am aware that there are numerous productive members of the sock monkey community who are not made from red heel socks. I do not mean to cast any aspersions in their direction with this developmental model, but rather suggest that the red heel was necessary to discover the presence of a monkey within two socks. All subsequent sock monkeys made from striped socks, argyle socks, etc., owe a debt to the red heel for pointing the way.

Through the decades, the shape, color, and method of manufacture of the red heel sock have gone through many changes. While monkey accoutrement also has changed over time, changes in heel really give an aspiring anthropomorphologist a chance to "cotton date" a monkey. For instance, the red area in the heels has shrunk in size over the years, so that while older monkeys have points on the ends of their mouths, modern monkey mouth shapes are much more like an oval. The "bell curve" of the monkey mouth is more extreme the further back you go. You will also notice that the older a monkey is, the oranger its mouth will appear. Whether this is due to fading or from a variation of original dye colors is again a matter that remains unsettled. One should note that the age of the genetic material does not indicate when the monkey in question was actually made. Vintage socks from the mid-twentieth century can be found today and turned into a sock monkey. Does that make the monkey a half-century old or was it born yesterday?

Sockosimians may have remained an underbubble in the "comfort creature" craftsphere had it not been

FOLIO FUN FACT

Regional and personal sock monkey variations are myriad. Googly eyes, embroidered eyes, felt eyes, button eyes . . . button noses, drawn-on noses, round noses, square noses. Mouth lines or not? Heel long side up or curved side down? Each and every one of us is recognizably a sock monkey, but the individual choices of our creators make us all unique. You may or may not have noticed, but I have three nostrils.

for two occurrences that resulted in a population explosion. First, Nelson Knitting started including the pattern for the sock monkey with every pair of socks it sold. This was the result of a legal battle for the patent on sock monkey reproduction techniques. A woman from Colorado claimed patent rights to the sock monkey pattern. She began taking actions to prevent other crafters, some of whom had active sock monkey businesses, from making monkeys without her permission. Concerned merchants contacted Nelson Knitting. Fearing a decrease in sales of socks to crafters, the sock company amassed a collection of monkeys and testimony from all over the country that predated the Colorado woman's 1953 patent. The pattern was declared to be a product of the "collective unconscious" and was awarded to Nelson Knitting for the sum of one dollar. Rather than exploit the rights ruthlessly, the company decided that selling as many socks as possible was a better goal than merchandising a potential company mascot, so they gave the idea away in every package.

Second, Nelson joined with popular midwestern craft magazine *Pack-O-Fun* to publish an essential work called *How to Make Sock Creatures (Come to Your House)* in the late 1950s. This slim tome detailed

COMMON FACIAL FEATURE VARIATIONS OF THE AMERICAN SOCK MONKEY

EMBROIDERED
PimPom

GOOGLES
Long Gone

BUTTONS
Phillipe L'Onion

EYES

FLAPS
Irie

SHAPED
Chica la Friqua

SHELLS
Harry Eyes

EARS

DOWN MOUTH
Burt

UP MOUTH
Little Prince

MODERN MOUTH
Overly Norvous

MOUTHS

REINDOG, SOCK DOG, SOCK ELEPHANT, SOCK KANGAROO

the many types and varieties of extant sock creatures and gave tips for attracting and breeding them. Revealing among other things that the sock monkey was only the toe of the sock-animal iceberg, the book introduced such exotica as the sock elephant, the sock kangaroo, the sock cat, the sock dog, the sock worm, and the sock octopus.* *How to Make Sock Creatures (Come to Your House)* is a virtual Genesis text for the sock monkey, and its importance cannot be overstated.

What, then, is our purpose in the great thread of being? We are creatures of comfort. It is our responsibility to relieve human children from anxiety and dismay and to provide companionship in their idle and not-so-idle hours. But unlike Beanie Babies or Tickle Me Elmos, we do not exist within market forces. We are, each of us, unique creatures, made by hand and gifted to children who may or may not want us but who sometimes come to feel that we are a

necessary part of their lives. Often, the devotion bestowed on us surpasses that shown to comfort creatures of a more commercial origin. Perhaps children realize that we are individuals just like they are.

FOLIO FUN FACT

For sock monkeys, reproduction can be a confusing topic. We depend on human beings to create us. Any sock monkey that denies this is just being willfully ignorant. Gone are the days when we believed we were brought to the world by sock storks. Without two socks, a needle, thread, a pair of scissors, and a person, there would never be another new sock monkey. How we have continued to perpetuate our species is another subject of debate. Sock monkey science states that our simplicity of design, uniqueness of character, and, most important, our delightful and charming nature compel people to make more monkeys. Others speak of "the Great Grandma," a higher power who guides the hands and hearts of all those moved to make monkeys. Whatever one chooses to think, human inspiration is key to our continued survival as a species.

*All sock octopi I have ever spoken with loathe the common appellation socktopus.

However, just as there are plenty of children who have no need for their sock monkeys, there are plenty of sock monkeys who have no need for children at all. Rejecting the traditionally passive comfort creature role, these monkeys leave their comfortable domestic confines, looking for fame and adventure. Rounders, entertainers, thieves, or troublemakers, they constitute a secret history of sock monkeys.

Take, for instance, the GAGA OSME* circus, which traveled throughout Europe and the Middle East in the middle part of the twentieth century. Led by Ollie George and featuring a group of riotous clowns, elephants, and monkey oddities, this improvisationalist troupe had a huge following, saw massive publicity in its day, and may have introduced country music to Europe in some of its merrier pantomimes. It is virtually impossible, however, to find documentation for the Cirque du Monqué. Its history is largely curated by Ollie himself.

JIMMIE BRAKEMAN AND BOXCAR BILLY POSE FOR THE COVER OF *BRAKEMAN AND BOXCAR SING FOLK SOCKS*.

Similarly, Baby Jane, a sock monkey actress of dubious talent, is said to have enjoyed a brief vogue in a series of movies featuring her singing, dancing, and outrageous sense of misbehavior. But while many sock monkeys can fondly and vividly recall scenes from *The Doll Who Saved Them All, Bread Line Baby Jane,* and *Monkey Picnic Panic*, these films are not found in any cinema texts.[†] This lapse in human memory is vexing, given firsthand sock monkey reports of Baby Jane films or reminiscences from GAGA OSME members that the bulk of their audience was human

EARLY BABY JANE PUBLICITY PHOTO

beings. I myself can recall the poster to *Socks and Stripes Forever* but can find no written record of the film.

For the most part, sock monkey entertainment has been created for other sock monkeys. Folksingers Boxcar Billy and Jimmie Brakeman, for instance, two Rounder Monkeys whose tales of independence, like "I Ain't Got No Family (and I Couldn't Be Happier Now No)" and "I May Have Been Sewed but Give Me the Road," inspired more than one monkey to leave its household. Discrepancies between sock monkey memory and human memory may also account for the sock monkey's absence in American popular and academic culture. We are not chronicled in any folk art encyclopedia of which I am aware, nor are we listed in toy catalogs ascribing collectible value to comfort creatures of the past. This stems from our strange position of being a comfort creature at the folk/commercial nexus. Promoted by the market forces of a sock manufacturing company but handmade by the grandmothers of rural America, we find ourselves in the unique position of being mass manufactured by the masses.

*The Great and Gregarious Aggregation of Sock Monkey Entertainers.

[†]Amazingly, both Baby Jane and many members of the original GAGA OSME troupe have survived to the present day and have taken up residence at the Red Heel Monkey Shelter. More on their history appears later in the book!

In the early 1960s, a study was undertaken by the human Reginald T. Whitbouy (self-described "unnaturalist scientist"), attempting to bridge the human/sock monkey divide. Titled *Garrulous in Our Midst,* the book hypothesized that sock monkeys were sentient and recommended that, although there was no apparent need to fear them (hence the title), it wouldn't be a bad idea to acknowledge them. Whitbouy was one of the first people to assemble a number of sock monkeys from different creators and

REGINALD T. WHITBOUY CONDUCTING A FIELD STUDY

to house them together in order to watch them interact. He spent years closely observing them, cataloging their differences, and trying to understand their mental processes. His book claims that sock monkeys live simultaneously in human reality as well as inside a kind of collective mutual dreamscape. While sock monkeys may be sitting wherever they physically are, they are also engaged in active internal fantasy experiences that are shared by all. The more monkeys placed in a single environment, Whitbouy theorized, the more realistic the shared internal landscape becomes.

Although this theory is fascinating, when Whitbouy published *Garrulous in Our Midst,* his family had him examined by a psychiatrist, who decided that Whitbouy's obsession had overtaken his reason and that it was necessary to send him to a hospital for closer observation for a few years. He was never heard from in a scientific capacity again.

By the late 1970s, population growth of the sock monkey was on the wane. By the beginning of the 1980s, we were almost forgotten, displaced to attics, bottoms of toy boxes, and trashbags full of old clothes. Why were sock monkeys so devalued by their former friends, the humans? I blame the mall. With the rise of the mall in the 1980s, general stores and work socks were replaced by sporting goods stores and tube socks. Consumer culture forsook homemade craft items for those that were brand new and store bought. If something didn't come from the mall, it wasn't any good. And sock monkeys don't come from a mall.

However, as with many things that pass from cultural memory, the sock monkey did not vanish—poof—into the ether once it stopped being useful.* Eventually we found our way from closets, attics, and basements into thrift stores, yard sales, and flea markets. As we emerged into these environments, we gained a new status. We were no longer a free gift from Grandma but something on a table, For Sale, to be impulsively, and usually affordably, purchased. As such, our cultural coin began to grow again. Sometimes we found ourselves in that insidious environment of stuffy oppression, the antique mall, where we were tagged, numbered, and displayed with entirely too much dignity. Give me a thrift store any day! I was, in fact, at a flea market when my current hosts bought me.

Our slow crawl back into the limelight has been aided by the reemergence of the red heel sock, this

*Nothing ever truly vanishes—it just gets put under the next layer of stuff. This is how fossils are formed.

time manufactured by Fox River Mills, who obtained the patent from Nelson Knitting. The socks have changed—the heel's shape is less expressive—but the ever-adaptable sock monkey has branched out into more diverse costumery and accessory detail than ever before. A new generation of monkey makers, perhaps inspired by the Great Grandma, has begun to make monkeys with a more self-aware, arty twist.

While renewed interest in sock monkeys may smack of nostalgia to some, I disagree. I think there is another explanation for the recent wave of human attention directed toward us. It is easier to identify with us than with other comfort creatures. We exist within a basic repeatable pattern that never comes out exactly the same way twice. Our personalities are formed by imagination, whatever raw materials happen to be at hand, random chance, and the ravages of time and the environment. These qualities make us much more human than the average toy.

But enough from me! On to Mr. Hathaway's book! In it, sock monkeys tell their own stories and share their own experiences and history as it has happened and as it is happening *right now*—a forward-looking community for whom the Red Heel Monkey Shelter is not a grand novelty, but simply a home. May the Redheels bring humor and wonder into your life, and may you then take these things into the world and share them in your own human, or monkey, way.

Thank you for your attention.
FOLFO

DID YOU KNOW???

Sock monkey dolls are dolls that look like sock monkeys, but they aren't really sock monkeys. One sock monkey doll can look exactly like another one. They usually come with tags sewn into them. Sock monkeys also call them preebles.

I would like to acknowledge the invaluable assistance of Dr. Dan Bartlett, curator of exhibits at Midway Village and Museum Center in Rockford, Illinois, and David Moxley, associate director, HMI Executive Programs, University of Missouri-Columbia, for their knowledge and research skills. F.

I HEARD IT THROUGH THE APE VINE

BY BENNY HATHAWAY

BENNY HATHAWAY

M name is Benny Hathaway. I'm a reporter; I write and edit a newspaper called *The Monkey Ape Vine* (*TMAV*). *TMAV* covers the daily events that go on at the Red Heel Monkey Shelter. As far as we residents can tell, the Red Heel is a sock monkey preserve. The last time I took Monkey Census, our population was 157 monkeys, 2 elephants, a cow, a bunny, 2 dogs, and a kangaroo. And one hoobajoob. At least, we think there's only one. We hope there's only one. Other things live here, too, but I only count things made out of socks. You have to stop somewhere.

Before we go any further I think that we should get one thing straight. The way the monkeys at the Red Heel Monkey Shelter look at life is not necessarily the way *all* sock monkeys look at the world around them. I am not writing a treatise about monkeykind. I think that individuals are more important than big questions about existence.* Any assumptions about how sock monkeys outside the Red Heel behave, based on the activities described in these pages, are to be made at the reader's own risk. Not all sock monkeys are self-centered, crazy, infused with magical powers, or con-

FOLIO FUN FACT

A hoobajoob is a mysterious supernatural being, something like a sock monkey vampire. According to legend, hoobajoobs move into houses where five or more sock monkeys reside. Purported to be sock monkeys who are "sewn wrong," the nasty, walleyed creatures carry around a pair of rusty scissors. Whenever a sock monkey falls or carelessly wanders to the floor, the hoobajoob scuttles from its hiding place, leaps upon its victim, and cuts him or her to pieces with its scissors. Whether or not hoobajoobs actually exist is up for debate, but most sock monkeys tend to err on the side of caution and stay well clear of the floor if they can possibly help it.

vinced they are royalty or ex-movie stars. Not all monkeys have their own TV shows, join rock bands, or run little secondhand shops. As far as I know. But some of the monkeys here do these things.

Each Redheel has an agenda to pursue and does so with a single-minded passion. Mrs. Tiffany, the Red Heel's alpha Kitchen Monkey (she claims she once belonged to Brian Wilson), sings loudly in the kitchen as she raids the cooking sherry. Olga, the superstitious gypsy refugee, puts a curse on somebody. Xantham Gumm, embittered by his years of servitude to a young boy who "branded" his name on the poor monkey's back, swears at his domino partner, Petey

---

*How am I supposed to know about "existence"? I'm only a monkey! I know about only what I have seen and what I have read in books. And as Folio told you earlier, there aren't a lot of books about sock monkeys.

XANTHAM GUMM

PETEY SWEETJAW

MOLLIE HAVERSHAM

OSCAR ONO

OLGA

Sweetjaw. Newlywed Mollie yells at her hapless husband, Oscar. Burt, the bathroom butler, welcomes guests to his "area." GB, owner of GB's Crazy Stuff Store—an emporium of dubious third- and fourth-hand goods, asks somebody, "What do you got that I can take?" Pierre Mon Frère and his band of Leetle Troublemaikers plot acts of sabotage.

But if you were watching us, you might not think we were doing very much—other than sitting on shelves, the tops of bookcases, chairs, headboards, the chorus board,* everywhere. But when I go from shelf to case to board, in my reportorial capacity, searching for stories for *The Monkey Ape Vine,* it turns out everyone has been very busy. We may look like we are just sitting here, but we're really getting stuff done. We're not just collecting dust; we're collecting experience.

BURT

MRS. TIFFANY

PIERRE MON FRÈRE

GB

*Peoples call this a cornice board.

MONKATYPES CHART

COMFORT MONKEY
Traits: Know lots of games and like to play (good companions). Don't mind being used as a pillow. May require constant maintenance. {Li'l Dinah}

KITCHEN MONKEY
Traits: Usually female, usually older, and always a little odd. Favorite foods include nuts, bananas, and crackers. {Aunt Lovey}

MISCHIEF MONKEY
Traits: Practical jokers, thieves, arsonists, deconstructionists, and signifiers. {Pierre Mon Frère}

BED MONKEY
Traits: Soft, squishy, and simply made. Ideal for snuggling; subspecies of Comfort Monkey. {Emily}

MONSTER MONKEY
Traits: Not necessarily evil or scary, but something about the way they were sewn makes them prone to rampages. {Pumpkin}

CLOWN MONKEY
Traits: In this case, form dictates function. {Starbo}

HERE ARE SOME TYPES OF SOCK MONKEYS WHO LIVE AT THE RED HEEL MONKEY SHELTER

MAGIC MONKEY
Traits: Possess supernatural powers originating from either ancient mystical wisdom or commercial holidays. {Silly Sally}

OLD WORLD MONKEY
Traits: Usually don fezzes or nonsock hats or otherwise reflect cultural costuming. May have been a member of the arisockracy. {Gypsy Davey}

ROUNDER MONKEY
Traits: Roamers, ramblers, and rail riders. These monkeys tend toward antisocialism. {Jimmie Brakeman}

MINIMONKEY
Traits: Minimonkeys are made from tiny socks; the resulting monkey may be a full-grown adult (like Freddie here) or a minibaby. {Freddie}

I can still remember the day that I came to the Red Heel Monkey Shelter, although it was not called that at the time. I started calling it the Red Heel Monkey Shelter later, and the name stuck.

Before I was taken to the Red Heel, I was hanging in a tree inside a great big building. I know it is pretty weird that I was in a tree inside a building, but that's how it was! The tree sat in the window of the building, and there were two other monkeys in the tree. One of them was Li'l Dinah. Li'l Dinah didn't talk much back then, which is a shock to anyone who knows her now. I didn't talk, either. We were both pretty freaked out. We were For Sale.

From what most monkeys who have been For Sale tell me, being a For Sale monkey is not like being a Comfort Monkey or a Kitchen Monkey or a Bed Monkey or a Monster Monkey. You are those things while you are For Sale, but mostly what you are is Freaked Out. It takes a while to overcome being For Sale. I've seen numerous new monkeys come to the Red Heel with a dazed expression, unable to talk, think, or answer questions. Having a price tag safety-pinned to your ear will do that to you.

I was For Sale in an antique mall. I was "Monkey 15," because my tag read, "Monkey, $15." Li'l Dinah was "Monkey 32," because her tag read, "Monkey, $32." Another monkey there was "Monkey 28." I don't know whatever happened to Monkey 28. He got sold to someone else. I also don't know how I knew these words and numbers, but I did. I guess I've always been kind of a reader. Li'l Dinah and Monkey 28 and I were in the window of the antique mall, in a tree, looking out at the peoples going by.

Hanging in the tree was uncomfortable. I don't have fingers and toes (which is making typing this very difficult, by the way), so I can't hold on to branches. I was sort of propped in the tree so that it looked as if I was hanging onto it. Instead, branches were sticking in my back and arms. I thought being put in a tree was pretty strange, since I am a sock monkey and am built for more regular surfaces. The peoples who ran the antique mall had put us there. They said we would sell quicker if they put us in the window. Then they decided to put us in the tree. Then they laughed.

I didn't hang there for long (even though it felt like munce) before some other peoples came in and pointed at me. I learned later their names are Reggie and Loretta.* The man behind the counter got me out of the tree. Reggie and Loretta said that I was a "good deal." They looked at Li'l Dinah, and Reggie said she was "too much." But they bought her later. Li'l Dinah is never going to let Reggie live that one down.

I liked Reggie and Loretta right away because they seemed so happy to see me. I know I said I wasn't going to make any sweeping generalizations, but I will say that I think deep down most of us sock monkeys just want people to be happy to see us. Reggie and Loretta said, "We'll take him," and that made me really glad because it meant I wasn't going back in that tree and I wasn't For Sale anymore. However, after they bought me, they put me in a plastic bag—and I hate going around in plastic bags (Redheels hate going anywhere in bags).

Pretty soon, though, I was grabbed around the tummy and pulled out of the plastic bag. I was in another place with lots and lots of stuff in it. But none of the stuff in this place was For Sale. It was a home, not a business. For me, the best things were what Reggie and Loretta called books. I remember Loretta saying, "I think this one's name is Benny. Benny Hathaway. He wants to go on the bookshelf." So they sat me on the bookshelf. Then Reggie put a book in front of me, and he and Loretta laughed and said I looked like I was reading. So they left me like that.

I watched Reggie and Loretta a lot, especially when they were using the books. My philosophy has always been "monkey see, monkey learn to do." So I did

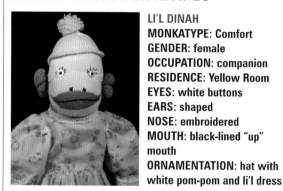

MONKEY CENSUS ENTRY #25

LI'L DINAH
MONKATYPE: Comfort
GENDER: female
OCCUPATION: companion
RESIDENCE: Yellow Room
EYES: white buttons
EARS: shaped
NOSE: embroidered
MOUTH: black-lined "up" mouth
ORNAMENTATION: hat with white pom-pom and li'l dress

what they did, and after some munce I was reading. Then I started understanding what I was reading. Eventually I was learning from what I was reading, too.

After munce of reading, I pulled my head out of my books. I noticed something I'd never really seen before. There were lots of other sock monkeys in this place with me. I don't know how I missed them. I guess I was too busy learning how to read. They were everywhere! On top of other shelves, on the couches and chairs, in the kitchen—everywhere you looked: monkeys! There was even a tall shelving unit with several stories, and each story held at least four monkeys.

I climbed down from my shelf and started walking around. I spent the rest of the day talking to some of the other monkeys. Everyone was very different and very interesting, but I discovered they, like me, weren't really aware of who the other monkeys were or what they were doing there. Some seemed surprised that another monkey was talking to them. Two or three were surprised that I was walking around. They asked me, "Don't you know about the hoobajoob?" I said I didn't. They said, "I wouldn't get on the floor if I were you." They all knew Reggie and Loretta, and everyone had different thoughts about them, but not about the other monkeys.

*Reggie and Loretta are the peoples who bring sock monkeys to the Red Heel. Most of the monkeys at the Red Heel have a lot of reverence for Reggie and Loretta (OK, at least for Loretta), and their affection is highly prized.

I noticed that all of the other monkeys had pastimes. One monkey fixed things he thought were broken (he usually broke them more, though). One monkey was happy only if he was put in a basket of clean clothes fresh from the dryer. One said he was working out. And one always said to leave her alone because she was "maintaining the structural integrity of the bed"!

This was the beginning of my understanding that some sock monkeys are just made (or inclined) to do particular things, and that they are most comfortable in particular places. In the wrong place, the monkey is unhappy. Some monkeys like to live in the kitchen. And Kitchen Monkeys have similar traits to each other. Some monkeys need lots of people attention and are always looking for snuggling. Some cause mischief. And some live in or around the bed. Bed Monkeys, in particular, seemed to have a certain status about them not accorded to other monkeys. I took in all this information and came up with the idea of Monkatypes, which are sort of like sock monkey species. Once we knew about Monkatypes, it was possible to make some unhappy monkeys happy by helping them find a proper activity or place.

MONKEY CENSUS ENTRY #57

MAMA ROUX
MONKATYPE: Magic/Kitchen
GENDER: female
OCCUPATION: psychic
RESIDENCE: in kitchen on the "toaster-to-tomorrow"
EYES: googles
EARS: shaped
NOSE: embroidered
MOUTH: unlined "up" mouth
ORNAMENTATION: matching hat and dress
MAMA ROUX PREDICTS:
"Some things gonna get better. Some things gonna get worse. And some things gonna stay the same."

MONKEY CENSUS ENTRY #23

UNCLE BOBO.
MONKATYPE: Magic
GENDER: male
OCCUPATION: wise monkey
RESIDENCE: Uncle Bobo's treehouse
EYES: black buttons
EARS: Tibetan ear handles
NOSE: embroidered French knots
MOUTH: half-lined "up" mouth
ORNAMENTATION:
pom-poms of many colors

I realized that I was the only monkey who could read, which made me a Reader Monkey. With a little more application and aping of the peoples, I discovered I could also write.* I decided I would start a newspaper to tell all of the other monkeys about what was going on. It was the question every monkey

*Learning to write with a pencil rubber-banded to the end of your arm is hard! It makes typing look like falling off a shelf.

BENNY

PATTI VALENTINE

TONY CICCONE

MRS. TIFFANY

AB SLEESTAK

EMILY

always asked me: "What's going on?"* I named the paper *The Monkey Ape Vine* because when I asked some monkeys about how they knew something, they said they heard it on the monkey ape vine. For example:

ME: "How did you hear about this place?"

PATTI VALENTINE: "Everyone knows about Reggie and Loretta. That kind of news travels fast on the monkey ape vine."

ME: "Tony Ciccone, how do you know that it's gauche to wear tail bows this year?"

TONY: "It's all over the monkey ape vine, Benny!"

ME: "Mrs. Tiffany, how do you know that Reggie and Loretta are secretly planning to cook us and eat us, and they're just fattening us up right now?"

MRS. T: "Oh, Billy, I heard it on the monkey ape vine!"

ME: "So, AB Sleestak, what do you hear on the monkey ape vine lately?"

AB: "What's the monkey ape vine? What's going on?"

ME: "Emily, how do you know that being the Number One Monkey is an awesome responsibility bestowed upon you by powers greater than our understanding?"

EMILY: "Go away. I'm trying to maintain the structural integrity of the bed."

I thought that *The Monkey Ape Vine* was a good name, so I used it for my newspaper. The problem was that none of the other monkeys could read it, and no one was interested in learning to read, either! I was publishing a newspaper for a community that could not read! I had to go around and *read* the newspaper to the monkeys who subscribed to it! And then I had to listen to them complain that I'd gotten stories about them wrong! Eventually, Lexington Whizz arrived and set up his Free Monkey Radio station, WOOH, and I got to go on the air every time *The Monkey Ape Vine* was published. Then I had to read it only once. I had visions of monkeys learning to read by following along with me while I read over the air, but to this day, I don't think a single sock monkey has learned to read because of *The Monkey Ape Vine*.

While I was going around reading *The Monkey Ape Vine* to my subscribers, I got the idea to take Monkey Census. I decided that if I was going to report on the monkeys around me, I should know more about them. So I went from monkey to monkey, asking questions. I asked about their jobs and their memories. I wrote down whether they had button eyes or felt eyes or googles (like me), if they had noses or not, if they had pom-poms or if they had ribbons. I asked if they knew anything about where we were or why Reggie and Loretta kept so many of us.

Getting answers wasn't easy. Flora and Schmendrick Hassenhüddle, for instance, are from the Old World, and they can barely speak any English. So I had to learn their language to take their census entry. Strangely, everyone at the Monkey House (we called it the Monkey House then) already kind of knew Flora and Schmendrick's story before I finally learned how to talk Hassenhüddlian. They knew that Schmendrick

---

*I understand that when peoples say, "What's going on?," it's kind of like saying "Hello" or "Greetings." Let me tell you right now, when a monkey says, "What's going on?," that monkey means it! Monkeys don't know what's going on! So be nice and tell them.

had lost his arm in the war, that someone had taken Schmendrick's arm "east" with them as a "war trophy," and that eventually Schmendrick's arm became known as "The Monkey's Paw" and that it was said to hold supernatural powers. Anyone I asked knew that Flora and Schmendrick were immigrants from the Old World who fled after Schmendrick's injury. How did they know? They heard it on the monkey ape vine! (I don't understand it, either.) Schmendrick was very bitter and angry. The only thing he'd learned to say in our language was "Keeck your ass!" Flora was very proud of her wardrobe. The only word she'd learned was *shoes*!

I also found from my interviews that this was not the first monkey shelter. Gail and Ginger, a really old couple who'd been with Reggie and Loretta for a long time, remembered that there had once been a Great Eastern Exodus in Trash Bags. Everyone had hated that.

GAIL

"Well now, I remember the trash bag exodus, heh heh! That were back in . . . well, it were a while ago. That boy and girl, they put pret' near everthing they had in boxes, and we were sittin' around on the boxes and wonderin' what was going on. This were at another house. An' then one day, they shoved us all in these black garbage bags! By golly neds, if you ever watched what usually happens to them black trash bags, that'd cause you some caution right there! So we're in the garbage bags, goin', 'What's goin' on? What's goin' on? What's goin' on?' and we're all pret' near sure we're livin' with the old coffee grounds and stuff, but eventually the bags got opened up and we were in another place, and there was that boy and the girl, and they were all smiles and happy to see us. So even though ever' time we get ready to move, we understand it a little better now and are a little bit less not likin' the garbage bags, we still don't like 'em all the way."

I decided that we must be in an animal shelter for sock monkeys, so I started calling the place the Red Heel Monkey Shelter, or the Red Heel for short. We call ourselves Redheels because of where we live, and some monkeys prefer it because the word *sock* has so many unpleasant puppetary connotations.

Since I was bought by Reggie and Loretta, the Red Heel Monkey Shelter has moved once, from a giant room they called a flat to our current location, which is called a house. A house has more than one room. It even has more than one floor. We went from one room and one floor to more than nine rooms and four floors. Now we can spread out and have plenty of space. Similar Sockosimians can gather together and live with their fellow monkatypes. Although we still all interact, each monkey can be in his or her own place.

After we moved, I still put out *The Monkey Ape Vine.* I did the layout on my Banana computer and took pictures with my digital elf. But my digital elf did a crummy job taking pictures, even though everybody said it was my fault. "You got me on my bad side!" said Baby Jane. "My arm hole shows in this picture," said Emily. (This was an especially annoying criticism since the story was about how Emily had a new arm hole.) "I'm out of focus!" "I look over-stuffed!" "My ears are too big!" And on and on.

Around this time I got a letter from a monkey named Folio. Folio had found a copy of *The Monkey Ape Vine* in a box of stuff. How he got it, I'll never know for sure, but my guess is that one of the Rounder Monkeys had discarded it while on the road (probably threw it away after he was done sleeping under it). Anyway, Folio was very enthusiastic about the newspaper. I still have his letter. He said, "Although the writing and reporting in *The Monkey Ape Vine* is of an extremely high quality, I have no-ticed that you may be slightly overextended when it comes to documenting your subject matter visually. I know of a photographer named Link whose skill with shutter and flash may be able to help improve the overall quality of your journalistic efforts immensely."

I contacted Link via the old-school monkey ape vine, and pretty soon he showed up on the Red Heel's doorstep armed with a vast array of lights, cameras, and energy. Link's pictures were so good that I made some monkeys do things again they'd already done so I could rewrite the story, this time with the better pictures.

It still really bugged me that nobody would bother to read what I wrote for the *Ape Vine*. Even Link wouldn't read what I wrote! Once he had taken a pic-ture, he was done with it. I finally decided that the main reason that books weren't written for sock mon-keys was that sock monkeys didn't read books. Peoples did. So I thought I would write a book for peo-ples. I asked Link if he was interested in doing it, and he mumbled something I couldn't quite understand but decided was a yes. So Link and I started compiling writings and photographs for this book.

Of course, once word got out via the monkey ape vine that I was working on a book, everyone had ad-vice about how to do it. No, actually, they had demands about how they wanted to be represented.

MONKEY CENSUS ENTRY #148

LINK RAY
MONKATYPE: Artist
GENDER: male
OCCUPATION: photographer
RESIDENCE: the studio
EYES: black buttons
EARS: rounds
NOSE: no
MOUTH: black-lined "down" mouth
ORNAMENTATION: hat with pom-pom, neck bow

MONKEY CENSUS ENTRY #1

EMILY
MONKATYPE: Bed
GENDER: female
OCCUPATION: maintains the structural integrity of the bed
RESIDENCE: the bed, stupid
EYES: googles
EARS: flaps
NOSE: no
MOUTH: unlined "down" mouth
ORNAMENTATION: hat with ribbon, neck bow, pajamas

When Emily heard about the book, she said to me, "Just make sure everybody knows who the Number One Monkey is." So, before I go any further, I should tell you that Emily is the Number One Monkey. Before there was a Red Heel Monkey Shelter, there was Emily. She started it. She was the first monkey that Reggie and Loretta got, and she had their attention to herself for a while. And she never lets anybody forget it.

A while after Emily left my office, Mace came in and said, "Mace hears you are writing a book. Make sure you tell everyone that Mace is King of Monkeys!"

MONKEY CENSUS ENTRY #3

STELLA AND JUNE
MONKATYPE: Comfort
GENDER: female
OCCUPATION: twins
RESIDENCE: Loretta's office
EYES: embroidered
EARS: shells
NOSE: embroidered
MOUTH: black-lined "down" mouth
ORNAMENTATION: matching jumpers, hats with red pom-poms

MONKEY CENSUS ENTRY #6

MACE
MONKATYPE: Monster
GENDER: male
OCCUPATION: king
RESIDENCE: the Big Room
EYES: gray buttons
EARS: round
NOSE: no
MOUTH: unlined "up" mouth
ORNAMENTATION: Mace needs no foolish foppery

I told Mace that Emily had already told me that she was the Number One Monkey. Mace said, "Mace has no concern for numbers. Mace cares who is King!" And then he pushed me over. So Mace is the King of Monkeys, but Emily is Number One.

Then Li'l Dinah came from the Yellow Room. She insisted that I print that she "rules the couch." She also wanted to let it be known that Bed Monkeys like Emily are not as good as Comfort Monkeys like Li'l Dinah, because Comfort Monkeys live in the front rooms where visitors can see them, but Bed Monkeys are hidden where no one can see them because they are (and I am quoting here) "ratty and smelly." So Li'l Dinah rules the couch, Mace is King of Monkeys, and Emily is Number One.

Then Stella and June hopped off their shelf and came to see me. They insisted that Emily was *not* the Number One Monkey and that they could prove it. I told them that if I had to keep putting in notes from other monkeys at the beginning, this whole book would be an introduction and no one would read it. They stormed off in a huff, saying, "We never get any credit!" So now Stella and June are mad at me. And everybody else is what I said they were earlier.

Instead of giving everybody space in the introduction, I want to go on with the rest of the book, because it's the rest of the book where everybody's stories, voices and personalities belong. What follows is a series of pictures that tell stories, and stories that tell about the pictures. Some are interviews, some are essays, some are tales. Some are excerpts from *The Monkey Ape Vine*. On a few, I was helped out by my cub reporter, Squishy, who you might find in some of the pictures if you look closely. But he's not in all the pictures, so don't strain yourself. By the end, you should have a pretty good idea about what goes on at the Red Heel. Not every monkey who lives here is going to make it into the book. That doesn't mean they're not important, it just means we couldn't find space for them this time around. It's each monkey's individuality that is most important, not the number of monkeys that live at a house or their cotton dating or any of that stuff, no matter how interesting that might be. I hope you enjoy the pictures and the stories and that you have lots of laughs. If you're not having fun while hanging out with sock monkeys, then you should probably hang out with something else. Thanks for reading! It's been a long time coming.

BENNY HATHAWAY

THE INNOCENT ARRIVES

onkeys arrive at the Red Heel Monkey Shelter in all kinds of ways. Some come home with Reggie and Loretta, who rescue abandoned sock monkeys from thrift stores, flea markets, yard sales, and antique malls. Some arrive in boxes—they are either sent by peoples who can no longer care for them, or they crawl in a box and mail themselves. Others simply show up on the doorstep. Peoples drop them off, or they make the daunting journey to the shelter themselves, braving the elements, playful dogs, precarious grates, and passing autos.

Once a monkey arrives at the shelter, everyone gives them some space. A monkey does not usually tell its name or do the things it likes to do immediately—there is usually an initial amount of shyness. Eventually, the new arrival tells its name and says what it would like to do. He or she might watch the goings-on at the shelter and join in whatever appeals. Or, another Red Heel citizen might take a newbie under his or her wing until the new monkey flowers into a contributing member of society. Some are content to sit around and watch the shelter go by.

The little monkey standing in front of the Red Heel is Sissy. She is very small, very young at heart, and at the moment she is very scared. All that Sissy has ever known about life is from living with little girls. Human girls. She used to belong to a little girl a long, long time ago, but eventually that little girl grew up and gave her to another little girl. Little girl number two's name is Myra, and she is Sissy's best friend in the world. But Myra is moving and has to scale down her possessions. With a great deal of sadness, it has been decided that Sissy will move to the Red Heel Monkey Shelter. "She belongs with her own kind," Myra's mom tells her.

Sissy doesn't know about that. She thinks that she's pretty happy with Myra. She's never given a thought to "her own kind" or thought that there might even be other sock monkeys in the world. She's never even really given much thought to her own identity. As far as Sissy is concerned, she is a happy little being living with another happy little being and that is enough for her.

So when she peeked inside the window of the Red Heel, she got quite a shock! So many monkeys! Everywhere she looks, there are other monkeys just like her.

If Sissy had a heart, it would flutter in her chest. She is still sad about having to leave Myra, but if she can't be with her peoples, at least she can be with her own kind. She stepped inside the house and dragged her little suitcase behind her to a rousing, choral "Hello!"

In her pretend heart, Sissy knows that she doesn't *really* live here, but it won't be a bad place to stay until Myra comes back.

THE SUBSTITUTE

Education is a controversial topic at the Red Heel. Some consider it a top priority, others think it's a waste of time, effort, and resources. Why they get upset over this "waste" is anybody's guess; it's not like they pay taxes.

Mrs. DeLala runs the Little Red Schoolhouse, and her approach to education is very practical. And patient. Attendance is sporadic, and students often need to be told things again and again.

"I try to encourage my students to articulate themselves," says Mrs. DeLala. "Many of my littler ones are very difficult to understand; their Speaklish is slurred and full of mispronunciations. And those Cool Girls, with their lingo, haven't helped matters at all. I tell the children: 'You will get your way more often if your listener can understand you.' The Little Red Schoolhouse teaches the three S's: speaking, socializing, and smarts."

"School is not so bad!" says top student Frannie. "We learn the munce, we learn the telling times, we learn the nine numbers and zero, and other things about thinking! There are games and other things to do! Mrs. DeLala is nice and pretty!"

Other monkeys feel differently. "Cheese Whiz!" exclaims Lenny. "I ain't gonna get no older or no bigger than I am right now! Does that mean I gotta go to school forever?!? I ain't doin' it!!"

When this picture was taken, Mrs. DeLala was suffering from a gaping seam split (a gaper) in her lower left flank. She went in for emergency stitches, and a substitute had to be called in. Unfortunately, since Mrs. DeLala had never been absent before, the substitute had to be selected practically at random.

The two male monkeys who bothered to attend class (Sparky George in yellow, Lenny in plaid) were sorely disappointed in the choice. The only reason Lenny ever comes to school is his secret crush on Mrs. DeLala. Given his druthers, he'd much rather be outside chasing butterflies.

But Lenny's plight was a minor one compared to Sparky's, because the substitute was none other than his *mother,* Mammy George! A self-conscious little fellow on the best of days, Sparky saw his mom come in the room, and he slowly wrinkled with embarrassment. It was bad enough that she had her Sunday-go-to-meetin' hat on, but she also wore a dress that showed her bloomers. And it was humiliating that she called him her little "spark plug." But the worst was when she got up in front of the class and said she was the "soostiboot." Sparky couldn't take it anymore. Pretending to take a deep breath, he raised his hand, knowing what he was about to say would get him in *big* trouble when he got home.

IT'S A STACTULAR SPECTACULAR!

Ladies . . . Gentlemen . . . Socks of all sizes! See before you the Sock Monkey Traveling Circus, Carnival, and Edutainment Extravaganza, the GAGA OSME—the Great and Gregarious Aggregation of Sock Monkey Entertainers!!!

I, Ollie George, racontrepeneur and announce-mentor, have assembled, for the amazement of peoples and 'panzees alike, the most exciting conglomeration of *Sockosimian* performers ever banded together for mutual purpose!

See Starbo as he pinwheels the perimeter of our stage with a speed and grace that is rapturous to the eye and vertiginous to the mind!

Hear the joyous exaltation when Cyrus Osirus performs his amazing juggling cymbals act! They clash in midair! They crash on the way down! They bash back in his arms, all in perfect time with different tones, playing a melody that would make Sach proud!

Marvel at the variety of nature's creations while you squint to see Freddie, the world's tiniest full-grown sock monkey! Witness his famous "Can Freddie Fit in This?" act, as Freddie squeezes his diminutized form into various containers supplied by the audience!

Gasp as high above the audience, Bumbo and Bubbles prepare for their controversial, but ever-popular, albeit controversial, kamikaze act!

But now, my friends, I ask you to turn your attention to the third ring of our stage, where the beautiful Princess Paloona,* our mysterious elephant dancer, performs her haunting and beautiful ballet! Witness the moving spectacle as she glides astride two powerful pachyderms! These delicately trained dolly mammoths fulfill the function of her feet, each dancing a carefully choreographed series of movements! Three beings unite and ten legs dance as one!

I speak truly, brethren and cistern, we are the GAGA OSME—and *you* will love our show!

*Sharp-eyed viewers may have noticed that the monkey atop the elephants is not the real Princess Paloona. This photo is a reenactment of a GAGA OSME performance, as no pictures of the original troupe, which toured in the '30s and '40s, are known to exist. During the shoot, Paloona, no longer as spry as she once was, fell from the elephants and injured her hip. Moffie, the Go-Go Poet Majorette, was hastily called in to fill her shoes and did a great job. The real Princess Paloona is feeling much better now. She can be seen in the photo as a member of the audience, sitting directly behind Cyrus Osirus, in her customary blue cape.

EMILY'S DREAM: A BED OF HER OWN

She sits in her room, stretched out, relaxed, comfortable, alone. Emily, first of the Redheels. She is poring over her book, her small plastic pupils scanning the words, understanding only one of them. She can't read much, but Emily can read her own name. For her, it's the idea of rather than the ideas in reading—it is the privilege of the Bed Monkey to while away the hours, head on a pillow and in a book.

Emily, the Number One Monkey, groundbreaker for the Red Heel Monkey Shelter, the alpha, the bossy, the relentless, the constant. Emily breaks the old rules to make sure they're still in place, forgets about the new ones because they don't matter anyway, and turns them all to her advantage. She had the shelter to herself once, and she has never quite forgiven any monkey that has come through the door since.

Now she stretches her arms, scratches the ribbon atop her hat, and surveys her bed, content. She peeks out the curtain to see a small gathering of monkeys down by the garden and sighs. Her thoughts turn, as they so often do, to structure.

"In order for a Bed Monkey, a Number One Monkey, a girl monkey to get any serious thinking done, to have any good ideas, and to maintain structural integrity, she needs a bed of her own and she doesn't need a houseful of monkeys screaming in her ear."

She yawns, feeling extra lazy, puts her book aside, and pretends to close her eyes. Then she awakes with a start, google eyes chittering around their clear plastic sockets like dice in a backgammon cup. No more single-size bed for Emily. She wakes up, back in a human queen-size one, with pillows that are bigger than she is. The bed is more spacious, but she must share the wealth.

Outside the bedroom, monkeys tear down the hallway in slug bugs, bicker over games of Slickety Wicket, and play their records loudly at all hours of the morning. All because of Emily. Sometimes One is the loneliest Number.

DID YOU KNOW???

Emily and Happy George are in a band called Bank & Hanger. Happy George plays the bank and Emily plays the hanger. Emily also has her own rap act called Public Emily.

ANYONE WHO HAD A HEART

Fauna and JD have been sweethearts since they met. Fauna is quiet, but JD is quieter. Most monkeys at the Red Heel are loud and active, but JD and Fauna's favorite thing to do is sit next to each other, snuggled up, quietly observing the world around them.

But just because they both like to be quiet doesn't mean they're completely alike. Fauna likes small, delicate things. JD loves big trucks and tractors. Fauna is an old-fashioned girl. JD is more of a modern monkey. JD loves to look out the window to see what is going on outside. Fauna likes to listen to what's going on around her.

JD doesn't speak, but it's mostly because he's at a loss for words. He can only say what's on his mind to Fauna. And Fauna loves to listen.

Despite his appreciation for heavy machinery, JD collects art. He tells Fauna that art is like a window to a different world. Fauna likes music as much as JD likes art. She tells him it is like a window, too.

JD thinks that Fauna is being silly—how can music be like a window if you can't see out of it? Fauna explains that a window is like a door you don't have to open. You go where it takes you in your head, but you stay where you are while you go. Anything that comes into your head comes in through a window, and your ears are on your head just the same as your eyes. JD disagrees. Windows go two ways; you can see out and out can see you. You can hear music, but music can't hear you. Fauna tells JD that now he is the one being silly.

Whenever JD comes to visit Fauna, he brings her something that shows how he feels about her. Sometimes it is something he made, sometimes something he found, sometimes something he bought. Once JD brought Fauna a painting he found. JD calls it *Bugs Play Jazz*. He thought it was a good painting, because it was like music for the eyes and art for the ears.

Whenever JD gives Fauna an endearment, Fauna puts on a record and the two of them sit and listen to it. She tries to make the music match the present.

Today, JD brought Fauna a valentine he made himself. He is very proud of it.

GOOD NIGHTS WITH HAPPY GEORGE

Happy George is one of the Red Heel's proudest sons. He's been a resident since the shelter's earliest days, and of all its citizens he is perhaps the most universally admired. Even those who grumble about the primacy of the Bed Monkey love Happy George.

"*Some* Bed Monkeys think their socks don't stink," says Monkey High-Rise superintendent Odd Job Jimmy John. "Not Happy George. So he got a big round head and little skinny arms and's stuff'd wit' squishy stuff. Great Grandma just made him a little cuter than most, but he don't let that give him a big head."

Happy George's cuteness is somewhat undercut by his fragility. He is more prone to back holes than any other monkey at the shelter. As his friend and fellow Bed Monkey Emily puts it, "Happy George has more back holes than whole back."

On his first talk show, *Happy in the Morning*, Happy George would interview the shelter's latest arrivals. He would become so engaged in their answers to his questions that they'd lose their self-consciousness. The show became an essential rite of passage for any monkey entering the developing Red Heel. *Happy in the Morning* gave the budding community a real sense of itself.

When the show moved to evenings (its morning schedule was breaking into Happy's valuable lounging time), *Good Night with Happy George* became more celebrity oriented. This created a need for celebrities, and a number of monkeys jumped at the opportunity. They soon became famous just for being regulars on *GNw/HG*.

This still is from the famous episode during which an invading spider monkey hopped on Happy George's head, interrupting exisensualist entrepreneur Sleazy Hugh's segment right in the middle of *Top Ten Sleazy Hugh Pickup Lines*.

The show's other guests that night included comedian Xantham Gumm (he performed his infamous bit, "the seven words you can't say to a sock monkey"), and a squeaking rubber hot dog.

Later in the episode, *Pantyhose* cover model Priss Patticakes stormed the set and beat the stuffing out of Sleazy Hugh, insisting that she had been promised her modeling was for charity. When asked what charity, she said Hugh said it was for "autistic porpoises."

"My interviewing style has always been the same," says Happy. "I ask my guest the first thing that comes into my head and act like the answer is the coolest thing I've ever heard. And then I ask another one. Pretty soon, I'm talking to someone who believes he or she's the most interesting monkey in the world, and then things get *really* funny. To tell the truth, I never even know what they're talking about. I'm too busy listening to remember what anyone is saying."

This technique is called Happy George-ing your way through a conversation, and you would be surprised how far it can get you in life.

THE SLICKETY WICKET

Every evening, Barney and Willajean go over to Harvey and Imogene's to play Slickety Wicket. It passes the time and gets everybody off the shelf. Barney and Willajean have known Harvey and Imogene since they met at a wedding chapel in Pigeon Forge, Tennessee. The couples were delighted to meet up with one another again at the Red Heel.

But it's a source of constant frustration to Willajean that every time she plays Slickety Wicket against Imogene, she loses. Willajean can't understand how it happens. She's *good* at Slickety Wicket, certainly better than Barney, who she thinks is dumb as a shoe. Willajean thought long and hard and finally came up with a plan to beat Imogene. Unfortunately, the plan required the help of Barney.

The object of the game is to stick the other team with the Slickety Wicket (the Queen of Spades). If Barney was on Imogene's team and was holding the Wicket in the last go-round, Willajean's team would win.

It was a good game that evening. Both teams won a couple of go-rounds and lost a couple of go-rounds. Then, at the crucial moment, with the score tied in the last go-round, Willajean passed Barney the Slickety Wicket! Now all Barney had to do was hold on to it until Willajean played down her four sets of threes, and Imogene would lose!

Would Barney be able to stick to the plan, or would he get confused in the pass-pass-trade round and pass the Wicket on to Harvey? Would Willajean finally beat Imogene, or would Barney blow it?

Let's put it this way: Barney slept on the porch that night.

RULES FOR SLICKETY WICKET
According to Willajean

Benny Hathaway asked me to explain Slickety Wicket to all you peoples. I hear tell that peoples hates our monkey games because the rules don't make no sense. But that's crazy! Even Barney can kinda play Slickety Wicket, and he's just 'bout a waste of material. Let ol' Willajean 'splain how you play.

You play Slickety Wicket with four monkeys. You got to pardner up. The object is to stick the other team with the Slickety Wicket. You stick 'em by being first to lay down your four sets of three: three in a row, three of a kind, three of a suit, and three faces. You can't use the Slickety Wicket in a set of three. Ev'ry time through is called a go-round. Three deals in ev'ry go-round. First deal is cut deal. Dealer cuts the cards and deals the number on the card cut. So if a six gits cut up, six cards gits dealt. Ev'rybody throws two of their cards into a pile in the middle of the table. This is called the Wicket patch.

Now the dealer deals the rest of the deck. Ev'rybody discards two cards in the Wicket patch and trades a card with their partner.

Third comes the Wicket deal. Dealer shuffles and deals the Wicket patch. When all cards are dealt, you can lay down whatever sets of three you got. Then comes the pass 'round. Pass a card to the left, a card to the right, and trade with your partner. You "pass-pass-trade" until somebody can play all their sets of three.

Whoever has the Slickety Wicket when the go-round is over gets a red chip. First team with seven red chips loses.

Now that's not so hard at all, is it?

THE SAGA OF BABY JANE

Baby Jane's movie career started without fanfare in a film called *The Funny Follies,* directed by Stanley Gollysocks. Although she was in only one scene, she stole the show with her soft-shoe shuffle tap and her "boisterous" singing voice. Positive reviews and fan response led to appearances in movies such as *The Doll Who Saved Them All, Monkey Picnic Panic, Breadline Baby Jane,* and *Socks and Stripes Forever*. These films were all low-budget musicals, and *Sick Sock* was to be her bid for stardom. In the end, the film's failure may have destroyed her career.

In *Sick Sock,* Baby Jane starred with the larger-than-ordinary Monster Monkey Orlo the G. When the good ship *Gollysock* blows off course, Baby Jane discovers the giant, voracious Sick Sock, played by Orlo the G. Sick Sock lives in near starvation, having consumed all the island's edible and inedible substances. Baby Jane insists that Orlo come back to the mainland as her pet. But back home she forgets to feed him, so he goes on a rampage and begins to eat New York City. Baby Jane, thinking her pet has run away from home, grabs a huge leash and runs off to find him, yelling, "I'm gonna get you back, Sick Sock!"

The president sends airplanes to shoot Sick Sock down while he is eating a rotating restaurant near the Empire State Building. When Sick Sock falls, Baby Jane runs through the barricades for her close-up as she mourns the death of her pet.

Problems with the filming began almost immediately. Baby Jane was deeply resentful of Orlo the G, who was getting top billing. She would not talk to Orlo, referring to him as "the prop." Matters were not helped by the fact that Orlo the G was a Monster Monkey, prone to mood swings and fits of unquenchable hunger.

The film did get made, but it was a dismal box-office bomb. This is partially attributable to its title (it sounds like a melodrama about a dying monkey in a hospital rather than a thriller about a monkey with a bottomless stomach). But blame must ultimately fall on Baby Jane. The general critical consensus agreed—her performance was difficult to comprehend, poorly acted, and just randomly odd. Her insistence on breaking into song at entirely inappropriate moments could not be edited around, and her refusal to take direction or even seek direction was obvious. And she used the phrase "You big ape!" incessantly.

After hearing about her divalike demands and witnessing her disastrous performance, no respectable director would hire her. She found work in films on the "B" and lower alphabet circuit. Still, she was erratic, maiming several actors while filming supposedly "improvised" escape scenes for *Killer Kidnapped Kutie*. Eventually no one would hire her.

But in her mind, Baby Jane is still a star, eternally awaiting her next big role. Even after she moved from California to the Red Heel, she still believed that her comeback was right around the corner.

COOL GIRLS SLUMBER PARTY

When the Cool Girls get together for a slumber party, all the boys better look out! What's in? What's out? Who's tolerable? Who's annoying? Only Minxie, Trina Lynn, Rabéla, and Nellie Bellie know for sure! Now, through the miracle of Spy-O-Monkey (Squishy with a tape recorder), we can finally hear what the Cool Girls talk about at their notorious second-floor slumber parties. Let's listen in, shall we? If you get confused, consult the wackypedia!

DɪD Yᴏᴜ Kɴᴏw???
Squishy appears in *Sock Monkey Dreams* 12 times.

Cool Girls Wackypedia, Vol. 1

Don't block the box—Go with the flow.

Fold you!—Get bent.

HiMain—High maintenance. Requires excessive attention.

Jamz—Songs. Also records.

Janky—Opposite of snitzy.

Less slow, more go—You're blocking the box.

Nerdist—Someone who goes around without any cool on.

NTBM—Not to be missed.

Quit trying to P-A me!—Don't use passive-aggressive techniques to motivate me, please.

ROTFLLACB—Rolling on the floor, laughing like a crazy baboon.

SBT—Strange but true!

STHU—Shut the heel up!

Snitzy—Cool, enjoyable, something to endorse.

What's snaggin' your sock?—What's the problem?

WTTT—Word to the third. "I surely agree with what you are saying! Emphatically!

Trina Lynn

Rabéla

TRINA LYNN: "Hey, DJ Rabéla! Sock it to us with that Question Monk song again! Shake your red red red! So good!"

RABÉLA: "Nah, that's the old news, TL!"

NELLIE BELLIE: "Yeah, Trina! This is not your mother's slumber party! Get hip to what the new breed say!"

TRINA LYNN: "Oh, fold you guys! I love Question Monk! He's rockaroll!"

RABÉLA: "I got a new jam in GB's dolla bin today. Check it! Lancelot Link an' the Evolution Revolution! NTBM!"

NELLIE BELLIE: "WTTT! Do you think Lancelot Link is any relation to Link the photographer?"

RABÉLA: "You mean that guy who keeps takin' snaps of us? Doubt it. Looks like Lancelot's a real monkey. Link's sock-type."

NELLIE BELLIE: "Link's pretty snitzy, though. He's got that scowl . . . Anyway, put on the jam! Less slow, more go!"

MINXIE: "Hhhmph! Link's stuffed full of himself!"

RABÉLA: "Minxie Bag, why you hhmphin'? What's snaggin' your sock?"

MINXIE: "I wanted Link to do a photo spread of me in different clothes for *Sockteen* magazine but he didn't want to! Hhhhmph! He said he only does art not ads."

NELLIE BELLIE: "Minxie—can you be any more HiMain? I'll bet you didn't even ask him! I bet you just tried to P-A him into it!"

MINXIE: "I did not! How do you expect anyone to keep chic if they don't have tips from the chic-keeper?"

NELLIE BELLIE: "Minxie, quit pooping the party!"

RABÉLA: "Yeah, Minx. Quit blockin' the box!"

NELLIE BELLIE: "Hey, Trina, your new skirt is nice! But somewhere out there is a very cold barstool."

Nellie Bellie

TRINA LYNN: "Shut up, Nellie! I saw you flirting with Benny down on the first floor today! Are you gonna ask him out?"

NELLIE BELLIE: "STHU! I can't help it if he has the best googles. Sigh. But he's a total nerdist! Signs point to 'No!'"

TRINA LYNN: "So who's cuter? Benny, Bolan, or, um . . . Barney?"

NELLIE BELLIE: "Barney!?!? You mean Barney of Barney and Willajean? That dude is OUT!"

TRINA LYNN: "OUT?"

NELLIE BELLIE: "Old, ugly, and terrible!"

ALL: "ROTFLLACB!"

Minxie

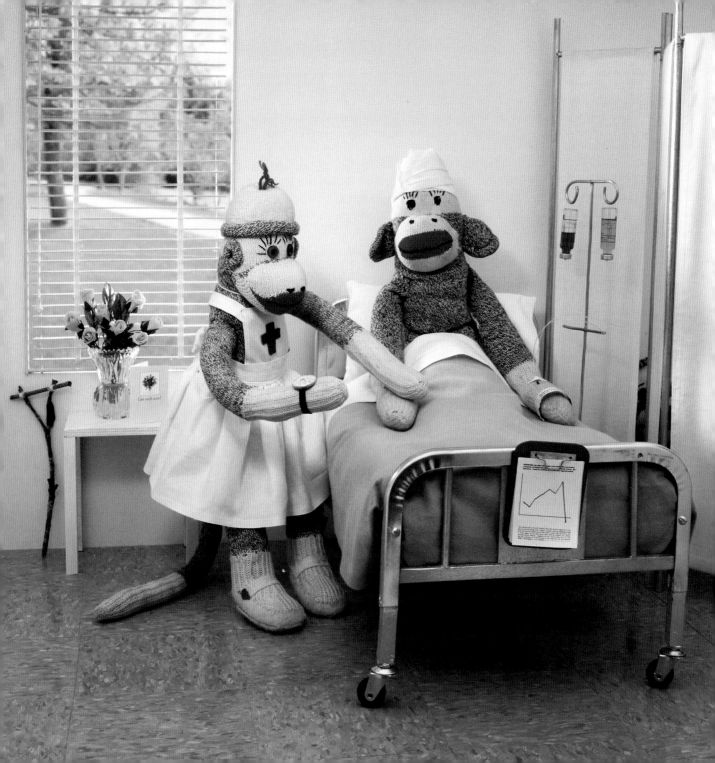

MONKEY REPAIR DAY
WITH BOO BOO BOB

Hi, everybody! My name is Boo Boo Bob! Nice of you all to come see me during visiting hours. It's Monkey Repair Day, so it's time again to talk about monkey maladies, preventions, and cures. I'm an expert. I've checked myself into the hospital for most of these things one time or another. I'm on a first-name basis with Nurse Dana, here. One very important factor that I cannot stress enough: When it comes to monkey maladies, a stitch in time saves nine!

Five Monkey Maladies and What Can Be Done About Them

1. HOLES—Back holes. Arm holes. Tail holes. Holes are the result of activity, handling, and too much movement. Some sensitive, thin-skinned monkeys are more prone to holes than others, but anyone can suffer a hole under the right conditions. If you get a hole, get it sewed immediately! It will just get bigger and bigger and bigger until you turn inside out!! A small hole is operable with just a little needle and thread—a bigger hole might require a graft.

2. RUNS/HERNIAS—Unchecked holes can also lead to runs. Monkeys may also be born with runs due to overstuffing. The runs are no fun and are painful and scarring to close. Hernias are runs in specific areas with partially protruding stuffing.

3. GAPERS—Gapers are the most common monkey malady, and the most easily treated. A gaper happens when a seam comes unstitched along the arm, leg, or tail. Unchecked, gapers could lead to much larger gaps and eventual loss of stuffing. Plus, it's considered bad etiquette to run around with a gaper showing.

4. STUFFING ROT—This condition affects monkeys stuffed with squishy yellow foam. In the old days, yellow foam was a very popular and frequently used stuffing. The negative results don't show up until many munce later. The foam can start to separate, and eventually it begins to crumble to dust. Symptoms include a powdery yellowish discharge, hardening of the stuffing, and a tendency to slump. Aside from being terribly unsanitary, stuffing rot can eventually cause you to shrink away to nothing internally! The only known cure is a stuffing transplant. *Warning:* An all-body stuffing transplant can lead to drastic changes in personality and should only be used as a last resort.

5. BLEED—Bleed usually happens during or after a washing. Sometimes the dye in the stuffing bleeds through onto the outside of the monkey. Bleed can also happen around the heel areas—the red in the heel can leak out into the white area, resulting in a permanent "Kool-Aid smile." This condition is inoperable.

Other common monkey maladies include dangleye (and its cousins danglear and detail), slumpbutt, leg creases, and the fade, which is a result of getting too much sun.

WHAT'S COOKIN' AT COOKIE'S COUNTER?

Keep the ball rollin', keep the ball rollin', keep the ball rollin' at Cookie's Counter!

Her name is Cookie. She's a young Kitchen Monkey, full of ambition. Most Kitchen Monkeys spend the day rummaging through the pantry and getting into the cooking sherry (like Mrs. Tiffany) or engage in mystical pursuits (like Mama Roux). Truth to tell, most Kitchen Monkeys Cookie knows seem kind of, well, crazy. Cookie yearns for a life that is more than sitting on toasters and microwaves. She's worried that if she doesn't find her own way, someday she'll go crazy, too.

So she's started a new career; she's decided to open a monkey diner: Cookie's Counter. There's only one problem—Cookie can't cook. Enter brash-talking (but secretly golden-hearted) short-order cook Hummingbird Wilson.

Hummingbird used to work at a Country Boy restaurant, but moved to the Red Heel when she was "'bout wore out." Cookie has coaxed her back into the business. Hummingbird isn't always convinced she made the right decision. It isn't a day at Cookie's Counter if Hummingbird doesn't shout out, "You know why I retired in the first place, Cookie? 'Cause I'm *tired!*"

Cookie's Counter sports a cast of eccentric but lovable regulars. Flirty old barber Blair always embarrasses Cookie with lines like "Thank goodness only the cup of coffee is bottomless!" That irrepressible and inseparable duo, sweet mush-mouthed Petey Sweetjaw and sour foulmouthed Xantham Gumm, spend their days drinking coffee and eating toast. And you never know who'll walk though the door. Why, one day, the Question Monk himself stopped in for quesaquilas!

Not content with her current customer base, Cookie's always concocting ways of drawing new patrons to her restaurant. This burning desire to succeed leads to hilarious misadventures, especially when her gimmicks to draw patrons combine with her control issues to confound the clientele.

"Everybody does breakfast during the day and supper at night!" exclaims Cookie. "But we're going to be different! We're going to have . . . Day Supper and Night Breakfast! Nobody wants to just order rice, so we'll call it *Snow* Rice! We'll have *tree-grown* bananas! And instead of throwing out old coffee, we'll sell it at a discount! Who wouldn't want yesterday's coffee? They buy yesterday's bagels!"

Despite her hang-ups, Cookie keeps the ball rollin', and somehow everything always works out. She's going to make it after all. Confused? You won't be, next time you go to Cookie's Counter!

LOOKING GOOD, MACE!

A PROCLAMATION FROM MACE, KING OF MONKEYS

(As dictated to Benny Hathaway)

Mace bids welcome to those who are reading about Mace! Mace knows his subjects love to read exciting tales about Mace the Great, King of Monkeys! Mace thinks rulers who use the royal *We* when talking about themselves are stupid. Mace is one of a kind, so Mace uses the royal *Me*!

Wherever Mace has gone, he has sung the tales of his incredible deeds, bravery, and adventures. Mace slew the Hoobajoob Horde with big rock and bare hands. Mace can pull tall trees from the ground with a jerk of his tail. Mace conquered the argyle army even though he was outnumbered three nines to one. And once Mace threw a teddy-baby polar-bear into an ocean of red paint, just to watch it dye.

Some monkeys call Mace's kingdom the Red Heel Monkey Shelter, but Mace calls it New Macedonia. Mace spends his days working out, keeping himself fit to defend his kingdom from usurpers.

When Mace is not working out, he likes to spend his time in high places, overlooking his kingdom. Mace goes into the biggest room in the house, the Big Room, and climbs to its highest point. Then he beats his chest, sings songs of his glory, and pops open a can of Red Mace.

Benny Hathaway thinks he is smarter than Mace and tries to tell Mace that there are other places higher than the highest place in the Big Room. Benny tells Mace that there is another floor above the Big Room ceiling, but Mace knows floors are always below ceilings. Benny Hathaway can be very stupid.

If Benny Hathaway wanted to be smart, like Mace, he would drink Red Mace! Red Mace gives the mind a mighty clarity, so you can be smarter than your fellow monkey, like Mace! Red Mace puts strength in your limbs, so you can be stronger than your fellow monkey, like Mace. And Red Mace in your refrigerator shows that you have superior taste, like Mace! If you ever feel weak, stupid, or inferior in any way (to any monkey but Mace!), Mace suggests you try Red Mace, king of drinks—the drink of kings!

Red Mace will not actually make you as smart as Mace, as strong as Mace, or prove that your taste is as good as Mace's.

DID YOU KNOW???

Mace and Mindy are brother and sister.

MOLLIE GETS MARRIED!

(An excerpt from *The Monkey Ape Vine*, Volume 7, Issue 4)

The Monkey Ape Vine is proud to announce the union of Mollie Haversham and Oscar Ono.

As regular listeners of *The Monkey Ape Vine* know, Mollie Haversham arrived at the Red Heel Monkey Shelter in her wedding dress, singing a song.

> *My name is Mollie and I'm going to get married.*
> *I'm going to marry the boy I get.*
> *My name is Mollie and I'm going to get married.*
> *But no one has asked me yet.*
> *He's going to have two eyes, and he's going to*
>   *have two ears*
> *and he is going to have a tail.*
> *My name is Mollie and I'm going to get married,*
> *married to a monkey male.*

Her plan clearly outlined in song, Mollie proceeded to drive everybody at the Red Heel nuts by singing it, plaintively, day and night, until finally it was decided that something should be done. So *The Monkey Ape Vine* started a contest called Who Wants to Marry Mollie? Three finalists were chosen: Burt (see Eyes, Ears, and Mouths Table), Mace, and Oscar. Mollie went out on three dates with each eligible bachelor and described the results to *Ape Vine* "readers." Then we held a vote to determine Who Got to Marry Mollie.

Burt, the bathroom butler, took Mollie to his job and talked about changing the paper all night. Voters decided that Burt was married to his work already and couldn't marry Mollie. Mace watched a movie and had popcorn. He occasionally looked over at Mollie and acted annoyed she was there. He wouldn't share his popcorn. The Red Heel voted and decided that Mace was married to himself and couldn't marry Mollie. Oscar gave her flowers and proposed by singing a song.

> *My name is Oscar and I want to get married.*
> *I want to marry the girl I met.*
> *My name is Oscar and I want to get married.*
> *And not just to win the bet.*
> *She's got two arms, and she doesn't have a nose*
> *but she has pretty button eyes.*
> *My name is Oscar and I want to get married.*
> *I hope that I win the prize.*

After hearing this song, voters decided that a guy like that deserved a girl who showed up at the front door in a wedding dress. So Oscar was declared the winner and got to marry Mollie!

The ceremony was performed in the Big Room by Brother Rich. Moffie, Mollie's friend and roommate, was maid of honor. Odd Job Jimmy John, Oscar's closest friend (they live two feet away from each other at Monkey High-Rise), was the best man. The reception was held in the kitchen, where a giant cinnamon roll covered in white frosting (provided by Cookie's Catering) was served. Mrs. Tiffany sang her medley of "Wind Beneath My Wings," "The Rose," and "You Are So Beautiful."

BLACKOUT AT MONKEY HIGH-RISE BLAMED ON "POWERS THAT BE"

(An excerpt from *The Monkey Ape Vine*, Volume 2, Issue 3)

Monkey High-Rise (MHR), located in the Yellow Room, experienced a blackout today. Monkey High-Rise comfortably fits eight to twelve on each of its five floors (depending on the size of the monkey) and has all the conveniences a sock monkey could want: a good view; a solid, even place to sit; and easy access to the outside world.

When the lights went out at MHR, you could hear the "what's going on"s all over the Red Heel. I grabbed my notepad and arrived on the scene as soon as I could. I got there just in time to meet Odd Job Jimmy John and Schneider as they were going into the basement. I tagged along.

On our way downstairs, Odd Job briefed me on some MHR history. "See, Monkey High-Rise used to be two buildings—Monkey High-Rise East and Monkey High-Rise West. They faced each other across the room. Ovuh there and ovuh there. But in the great rearranging of whenever it was, Monkey High-Rise was joined together. But who knows how long it's gonna last? That's the thing with Monkey High-Rise—powers that be might move the whole thing on you without a moment's notice."

"You think it's easy runnin' this place?" Odd Job continued. "It isn't! Monkeys callin' me up alla time with crazy problems. Somebody called me yesterday because their water wasn't running! I said, 'Of course your water isn't running—you don't have running water!'"

We arrived at the basement, and Odd Job and Schneider started looking around on the floor. "If you can't fix a job using stuff lying around on the floor then you aren't fit to call yourself a handyman!" said Odd Job. Soon, likely looking problem-solving utilities were gathered, and it was time to figure out what was going on.

Odd Job thought for a minute. "Since there's no power, I bet one of these power boxes is broken. I guess we should take them all apart and see which ones are working. Schneider! Grab that screwdriver and start taking apart the boxes."

"Hey, Jimbo," said Schneider. "This looks like it might be your problem right here!"

"How many times have I told you not to call me Jimbo? You can call me Odd Job, or you can call me Mr. Jimmy John, but I ain't no Jimbo! Hey, you're right! That's not supposed to be sparkin' an' making explosions! Looks like we found the problem. Another success for the maintenance monkeys at Monkey High-Rise!"

It was later discovered that the lights went out at Monkey High-Rise because "the powers that be" had turned out the lights in the Yellow Room. Closer investigation revealed this happens a lot.

THE WINDMERE TREATMENT

While some Red Heel residents are newly made, most have quite a few munce on them. And the munce haven't always been kind. When a Redheel is feeling stretched tight, worn thin, or out of shape, it's time to go to RaFreshe, the Spa for Socks, to get stuffing realigned, wrinkles righted, loose strings tightened, and stray threads snipped, all in a relaxing and professional environment.

Minxie, the "hands-off stylist," gives the initial consultation. "We get a lot of older clientele here, and they can be very frustrating! They are usually interested in what I have to say about getting their shape back, but they don't like it when I criticize their symmetrical integrity! They say 'so what' if one arm is longer than the other or if an eye needs to be relocated. And they always refuse to change their clothes! Some of their outfits are really out of style! I have a whole boutique of the newest fashions, and nobody ever uses it. Hhhhmph! I am a newer monkey girl! I was born in a store! I don't understand how somebody could be so antishopping!"

After analysis and diagnosis, most of the actual work at the spa is done by old-school aesthetician Rabéla.

"Minxie don't really like touching the other monkeys," Rabéla explains. "That's cool, though. Patrons mostly come to RaFreshe for the Windmere Treatment, and I'm heel on wheels with the Windmere."

"Windmere is the third word of the whole RaFreshe experience," says Rabéla. "See, sock monkey skin tends to pill up, particularly in the mouth an' the rear heel area. Makes for that not so Freshe feelin'. Windmere is one fearless de-pill-atory device—a couple passes and you feel like you just come outta the loom."

In addition to Windmere treatments, the spa spruces ribbons, fluffs pom-poms, and shifts stuffing. Settling is a serious issue; everybody knows the truism: The older you get, the lower your stuffing goes.

"We use hot ironing stones to loosen the stuffing for easier shifting," says Minxie.

"No one needs to walk around the monkey shelter with Popeye arms or beavertail," says Rabéla. "But you got to make sure your shift stays shifted. After chiropractice, we suggest an exercise regimen to stop resettling. Basic stuff. Hanging upside down. Not sitting in the same place 'til somebody moves you. It's amazin' how few sock monkeys do that."

While some say RaFreshe emphasizes surface appearance over deeper character traits, Rabéla disagrees. "It isn't prideful to walk around lookin' like a refugee from a flea market. Even if that's what you are. We're not sayin' outside looks trump some more of that inside soul, but only a two-dollar fool thinks you can't get to B from A, right? Don't block your own box."

Both Minxie and Rabéla point out that there is a yoga studio, *elasticity*, right next door, for the monkey seeking to work on its inner health. Its instructor, Viparíta Karanī, is featured on the cover of the latest issue of *Comfort Monkey*.

We know that there are as many ways to play Slug Bug as there are bugs on the road. Red Punch Buggy. New ones are verboten. No returns. Two for missing. Dealerships don't count.

But no matter how you play Slug Bug, the why is the same. You get to hit the heck out of someone whenever you see a Volkswagen Beetle.

Perfected over thousands of miles of driving, Li'l Dinah and Samantha Brown's Slug Bug game has as many rules as chess, gets better mileage than crossword puzzles, and holds its value as a car game when Road Sign Bingo and I Spy have worn out their welcome.

So get in on the game that's assaulting the nation. Because the chance to slug someone in the arm when you see a slug bug is worth the hours spent staring at the road waiting.

LI'L DINAH

HOW DO YOU PLAY SLUG BUG?

SAMANTHA BROWN

LI'L DINAH: "Hi! This is the where we tell you the real and true Rules of Slug Bug! Ah'm Li'l Dinah and this is Samantha Brown!"

SAMANTHA BROWN: "I'm Samantha Brown."

LI'L DINAH: "Ah already told them that! Now ah am goin' to tell them the rules of Slug Bug! And you are gonna shut up and listen because you need to be reminded, too!"

SAMANTHA BROWN: "I do not, dangit. I know 'em just as good as you do."

LI'L DINAH: "That's sad to know. Now you got no excuse that you always *lose*! There are more rules than ah'm going to say, but these are just the basics. Old-school bugs are worth *two* points! If you see an old-school bug you shout out, 'Slug bug! Old school! Two points!' and hit the other monkey and say the score. If you don't say what kind of bug it is *or* you don't say the score, you don't get points and you can't slug! If the slug bug is an old-school convertible with the top down, you have to say, "Slug bug! Old school! Top down! Three points!' and then punch, then you say the score.

SAMANTHA BROWN: "New-school slug bugs are worth only one point. If you see a new-school bug, you have to say what kind of bug it is by saying its name. It gets its name by what color it is. Red ones are Ladybugs. Green ones are Moon Buggys. Gray ones are Plain Grains. White ones are Baseballs in the sum-mer, Snowballs in the winter. Yellow ones are Baby Short Busses. Blue ones are Smurfs. Black ones are Cockroaches. So if you see a Moon Buggy, you have to say, 'Slug bug! Moon Buggy!' and then you hit Li'l Dinah and say the score. If you don't say the right color or the score, you don't get the point. New-school convertibles with the top down are worth two points, but you have to say 'top down' to get them."

LI'L DINAH: "Every Slug Bug game goes to five points! First to five points wins! Then you start over! That way if you are playing with someone who is terrible, like Samantha Brown, you don't get so far ahead of them they quit! So you can keep sluggin'!"

SAMANTHA BROWN: "If you are driving around your neighborhood, and you know where there is going to be a slug bug because it's always there, you can't hit on it. If you see it and it looks like someone is going to hit you on it you say, 'Lives there, doesn't count.' And then it doesn't count. The first time you see it ever at its house, it counts even if you can tell it lives there, so you can hit on it. A slug bug only counts one time in a day. And dealerships don't count."

LI'L DINAH: "Those are the basic rules of Slug Bug! There are more rules, like Today's Special, and the Minus Bug, and bugs that have antlers, and tails, and bras, and nametags, but you can probably figure it all out for yourself! That's it! Tough luck and hard sluggin' from Li'l Dinah and Samantha Brown!"

BOWLING WITH BOLAN: GUTTERBALL OR TURKEY?

(An excerpt from *The Monkey Ape Vine*, Volume 4, Issue 6)

Sock monkey games are played one on one or two on two. Sock monkeys can't play team sports. When they try, the teams always argue among themselves about the rules of the game! Even sock monkey teammates can't agree on what the rules are. Any attempt at team sports turns into an afternoon spent arguing over the rules, and nobody ever gets any playing done. It's a fine way to spend an afternoon, but it's not very sporting.

Bolan James Junior would love to have his own bowling team in a nice league. He's made a bowling alley over by Mace's workbench. He's even printed up his own bowling shirt, with his team name, Red Heel Rollers, on the back. But he can't get a league going or even find one opponent. He's so much better at bowling than anyone else, no one wants to play against him. All the monkeys who signed up for his bowling league wanted to be on his team, and the Red Heel Rollers didn't have any competition. On top of that, in order to make the ball return work, Bolan had to build the alley on an uphill slant, so it's really hard to play.

Like any monkey who has risen to the top of his chosen field, Bolan has decided to have a go at the entertainment industry. He wants to do a sports show called *Bowlin' with Bolan (with Bolan James Junior)*.

"Since there are no other bowlers at the Red Heel, I will have well-known citizens come on the program and bowl with me. I will win, of course, but there's no harm in that. While we are bowlin', we'll talk about bowlin'. We'll say stuff like, 'Nice ball!' and 'I'm warming up now!' and 'You were robbed!' Natural bowling conversation. And then I'll have a different guest on the next time, and I'll beat him, too. I think it's a natural winner. I hope to get the lead-in spot before *Good Night with Happy George.* I hope to get the Question Monk to come on the show. Or Ollie George. Maybe even Baby Jane! And I have a theme song!"

Bowlin' with Bolan (with Bolan James Junior)
Bolan is goin' bowlin' today.
Bowlin' with Bolan (with Bolan James Junior)
Bolan's in the bowlin' alley bowlin' away!

"My father, Dennis John Junior, was a great tennis player," explained Bolan. "My brother, Rolf George Junior, plays golf. The Juniors are great monkeys for sports."

LOVE GROWS HERE

FLOWER BEDS AND MINIBABIES

(An excerpt from *The Monkey Ape Vine*, Volume 5, Issue 5)

Lily, along with her partner, Mindy, minds the shelter's three minibabies. Minibabies are a strain of Minimonkey that are not only small but are also perpetually immature. Left to their own devices, these little creatures have virtually no life expectancy. They are small and easily lost, and they are locked in a state of arrested infancy.

"Minibabies are the sweetest things," says Lily. "They're so affectionate and fun to be around, and they're really impulsive and natural. But you have to watch 'em close because they don't have a lick of sense and are real curious. You turn around for a minute, and they've fallen in a mole hole or, worse, some bird unthreads the poor darlin' to make a nest. Inside, you gotta keep 'em off the ground so they don't get hoobajoobed."

Mindy is the main caregiver of the trio of minibabies, while Lily is in charge of gardening and philosophizing. Ordinarily a woman of few words, Mindy becomes quite sparkly when talking about her "kids." "Bonky is boldest! He is always running off. And even though he is little, he is fast! If he starts to run, I am in trouble catching him! BeBe (sometimes we call him Marker Mouth when he is in trouble) follows Bonky but is less brave. Poor little Primi is scared and stays closest to me. That's OK, though! He is the softest and squishiest of them all so is funnest to hold!"

"Mindy and I believe there are alternative ways of doin' things," says Lily. "A lot of sock monkeys I know have a phobia about going outside. Because you can get dirty and you can get wet and you can get lost. But there's more to existence than sittin' around on the shelf. So we are proposin' more natural lifes. Like instead of usin' detergents and soaps to freshen up, we think you should just go out in the sun. The sun's got magical properties—it's nature's air freshener. It's true that you can get the fade if you stay out too much, but that doesn't mean you gotta be afraid. Just monitor what you're doin' and make sure to get in some shade from time to time. I wear a sunbonnet, myself.

"I'm really worried about the new generation of sock monkeys that are growin' up in this day and age," she continues. "They got so many synthetic fibers and they're stuffed full of that polyfill stuff. They never really know how it feels to be natural. I am worried for their health. We gotta stay connected to nature and we gotta take care of the next generation, because children and flowers are better'n grown-ups and weeds."

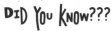

DID YOU KNOW???
Lily and Mindy are in a same-shelf relationship.

ODE TO THE OLD WORLD

FOLIO FUN FACT

Sock monkeys offer little help in clarifying their geographic and temporal origins. Easily confused by the concepts of time and distance, a sock monkey's sense of its personal history is sometimes difficult to reconcile with an established timeline. Personal reminiscences make claims for families and dynasties dating back to the seventeenth century or before, a historic impossibility for a species less than a century old. Similarly, some sock monkey narratives contradict their apparent all-American origins, claiming nativity to countries far across the ocean and indeed some locales not found on any map. These are the Old World Monkeys—a fascinating monkatype.

HELGA: "Ach! Heiney Shnitzel! You haff drunk der whole keg uf beer vor zee Soktoberfest! Zumorrow comes Flora und Schmendrick Hassenhüddle und Gypsy Davey und his Großmutter Olga! Ef there is nut beer, Schmendrick vill be grumpy und Olga vill curse us! Vut problems vor your poor Helga Schnoodle you have been makink!"

HEINEY: "Siggy Socky Siggy Socky hoi hoi hoi!"

HELGA: "I haff spend many days making die sokvurst und teachen der kindermonks to do zee chicken dance! Und now du ist dansing and singing und moving about like ein chicken vit no head. Now vut vill become uf us?"

HEINEY: "Wir drooken und drooken until our zocks / are vull to die pores / und zen wir vring ourselfs oot / und drooken undt droonken zum more!"

HELGA: "Ve haff no time vor your quaint oafish toasts, Heiney! Ve moost find zee new keg uf beer or ve vill nut be able to celebrate zee legendary ride of Princess Therese von Sock sen der High lederhausen on zee beck of zee doberman to meet her true liebe!"

HEINEY: "Princess! Princess! Princess Sock sen! Your hosen are zo high! Princess! Princess! Rise zem high-ah until ve can see die sky!"

HELGA: "I am hating zat chant more than oll uf zee others, I think!"

HEINEY: "'Elga! Look! I haff this year putten in der extra keg, because of last time, ven somevun droonken die keg on his own! Haben kein fear, meine liebchen! Soktoberfest is forever safe!"

HELGA: "Ach! Heiney! You giff me zuch ze start! But thanks to your long-range planning, you haff save Soktoberfest from yourself!"

HEINEY: "Ja! Now sing vith me, meine schatz, und heff a toast! Ve will only slightly tep this new keg!"

HEINEY UNDT HELGA: "Old vurld! Old vurld! Our mugs are raise to you! Vithout you ve vould nut exist! To you ve vill kep true!"

LEISURE ISLAND

Cleetus Crusoe dreams of sleep. Cleetus can sleep anywhere, at any time, on anything—nothing is too rough, pointy, or cramped. A chair, a box, a lampshade, a doorknob, it's all the same to Cleetus. Put him on it, and he'll fall asleep. If it's quiet.

For Cleetus, sleep is a goal, an achievement, an end in itself. Consequently, life at the Red Heel Monkey Shelter has become an irritation for him. As the population at the Red Heel has grown, finding a quiet place to sleep has become increasingly difficult.

One day, desperate for an early afternoon nap, Cleetus was delighted to find an unassuming brown barrel lying in the Big Room. No monkey was in or around it. He crawled all the way in and all the way down and was asleep faster than you can yawn.

However, this was no ordinary barrel. It was Captain Heelhead's booty barrel. Heelhead is a pirate. He sails the Sarabeeyum Sea in search of intellectual property rights to plunder. When he spies a good idea, he throws it in the booty barrel for later. The barrel had been placed in the Big Room temporarily by Heelhead's first mate, Flopsy Topsy Poopy Pants. Shortly after Cleetus crawled in the barrel, it was loaded onto their boat, the *US Mail*. They then launched the ship and sailed the Sarabeeyum Sea.

Cleetus's sleep was deep and untroubled by the free-floating ideas lingering in the barrel—not even dreams can interrupt Cleetus's slumber. The Sarabeeyum is a notoriously stormy sea, and on this particular voyage a vicious Black Funk buffeted the *US Mail* and sent the booty barrel over the side, into very murky waters. Thousands of stray ideas returned to the depths of the collective unconscious, but not even the raging storm could disrupt the first decent sleep Cleetus had had in as long as he could remember.

When he woke up the next morning, Cleetus found himself stranded and alone on a tiny island of contentment in a sea of turbulent confusion. The isolation, the utter lack of creature comforts, the closeness of quarters—it would be enough to drive a normal monkey mad.

Of the ideas left in the barrel, one of the oldest was a small bottle and a little piece of paper. Cleetus took up a quill pen and began to write.

Dear Whoever:

Don't Save Me!
I am fine!
I'm TIRED!
I just want to stay on my island!

Love,
Cleetus Crusoe

He sat back on his beach and tried to decide whether he was going to send the message or not.

HAPPY 434033

PIN THE TAIL ON THE ZIPPY!

From Bolan James Junior

ZIPPY'S BIRTHDAY PARTY

(An excerpt from *The Monkey Ape Vine*, Volume 2, Issue 8)

I was in the offices of *The Monkey Ape Vine* when I received my invitation to Zippy's birthday party. It seemed like only yesterday that Zippy was celebrating his birthday. Wait a minute! It *was* only yesterday! How did Zippy even know it was his birthday? Few monkeys can pinpoint what day it is, let alone remember when they were born. I thought about it and realized Zippy was throwing birthday parties daily! Maybe more than one a day! Had I discovered some sort of gift-scamming conspiracy? I grabbed my notebook and set off to get to the bottom of this.

The crowd was sparse. Not surprising. It takes the pressure off attending birthday parties when they happen every day.

I asked Zippy if he celebrated his birthday so often so he wouldn't miss it when it really happened.

"Everybody celebrates their self at a particular time, but nobody ever celebrates time's own self!" said Zippy.

This made no sense, but I carried on. "Why do the numbers never match up? One day you're eight-three-seven-five-five-two, and the next you're four-three-four-oh-three-three?"

"Consecutive numbering systems are extremely interrelated," replied Zippy.

"But is today really your birthday?"

"Did you know that the life expectancy of a minute is exactly a minute?"

Getting nowhere, I decided to chat with the guests. The Goofy Woopus was anxiously eyeing the cake. But the Woopus only speaks in piano triplets. He was no help.

Next I talked to Fat Randy, a regular cast member from *People's People*. Fat Randy never missed a Zippy birthday. I asked him about Zippy's parties.

"Are you *interviewing* me*?!?* For your *news*paper? *Wow!!!* That's great! I'm honored! You've got to tell me when this is coming out so I can get extra copies!"

I asked if he had an answer to my question.

"I knew when I got up that it was going to be a *good* day! I'm so *excited* that you are talking to me!"

Next I asked fidgety Harpo Z, the curly-headed monkey in the lion mask, the meaning of Zippy's constant parties.

"Keep a clear head and always carry a lightbulb!" he replied.

Seeking saner ground, I ambled over to the Velvet Frog, who was doing warm-up exercises on the mic.

"I just entertain, baby!" He winked. "I come, sing a few bars of 'Happy Zippy Toot Toot,' and scoot!"

Zippy came back to me and walked me over to a timer in a top hat sitting on a barstool.

"You can't beat the clock!" yelled Zippy. "Look! Ergonomic 'S' knob!" He pointed to the handle. "Ergonomic 'S' knob!"

Then he handed me something large, plastic and white. *"Giant spork!"* he yelled. *"Giant spork!"*

And the attendees at the party all started chanting, *"Giant spork! Giant spork! Giant spork!"*

I fled the party in a panic, glancing over my shoulder in time to see Zippy lighting the fuse on his famous exploding birthday cake. I knew when it hit the center that his birthday would be all over. Again.

'68 STARTUP: THE STORY OF THE QUESTION MONK

**(From *The History of Sock and Roll,* edited by Greil Monkus.
Transcript from an interview with the Question Monk, the king of sock and roll.
The interviewer never actually got to ask any questions before the Monk got rolling.)**

Hey, babay! *Woo!* This is the Question Monk, babay! Rock-a-rolla monk-a-tolla extra-ordi-nola-dola! *Yeah!* Gettin' down in red, white and brown! I'm so *loud* I make 'em scowl with my howl! I dance so fine, I blind with my *Grind! Ow! Get it!*

I know what you thinkin', babay! You wonderin'—"What it was like to be on the scene, to be a sock monkay back in the day when the Question Monk first got up to *play*!?" *Yeah you are!* Well, lemme tellya, Tiny Tina! Lemme lay it on ya, Little Louie-Lou-eye!

It useta be *all square and no dare* in Monkey Land! All sock monkeys were nothin' but a buncha little yarn-danglin', pom-pom-wearin' sit-on-its that would only have fun if some kid was droolin' on their arm or draggin' 'em through the mud by they tail! *Oh yeah!*

But then the Question Monk came along, and he had the *power!* He had the rock-a-rolla, and the rock-a-rolla let him *do* what he want, *say* what he want, and *be* what he *is* any time he want to *do it, say it,* or *be it*! Can I get a *"Right on!"*?

An' the Question Monk, he get up on the stage, an he let loose with his might-tay roar, an' all the monkeys, sittin' on their shelfs, they say, "Huh?!" And I say, "That's right, little monkay!" And they say, "What?" And I say, "You know what you got-ta do, don'tcha?" And they say, "No." Because monkeys back then, they weren't too hip to the harangue-utang.

And so I say to them, "You gotta shake *your red,* babay! *Woo!* Get up off it and wiggle!" An' then me and the boys'd kick in to "Shake Your Red!" And it was gooooooooooood! *Woo! Hot!* An' some of the brave monkays, they come down to the stage, an' they look up at me shakin' my red an' singin' my song! An' they start to move a little bit, loosen up a little, wigglin' they arms, movin' their heads, an' even shakin' a little red. An' more an' more monkeys come to the shows, an' pretty soon when I sang "Shake Your Red!" there was full-fledged fever-flingin' *frenzy*!

So that's how it *was,* babay, an' that's how it *is*! To this day, whenever you hear Question Monk singin' "Shake Your Red!" you better get up offa that whateva you on, throw your hands in the air, and *shake* that red. Either that, or you betta off dead!

And that's what I'm talkin' about!

Lata, babay!

DID YoU KNOW???

**The Question Monk's biggest hits are "Shake Your Red," "Monkey Pile," "Red Heel Rock,"
and "Get Off of My Back."**

IT'S FUN TO LEARN AND SING A SONG!

My name is Mr. Poople!
I will take you to schoople!
It's fun to learn and sing a sooong!
If not, you will be stoople!

All little boy and girl monkeys recognize the theme song to *Poople's People*, the top-rated monkey-kid's program created and hosted by Mr. Poople.

To Mr. Poople, the whole world is a magical place of learning and discovery—a great big beautiful bow just waiting to be undone, if only so he can learn how to do it up again. Largely self-taught, Mr. Poople encourages monkey-kids to, above all, think for themselves to discover how things are. He likes to tell the little girls and boys: "You can learn anything by looking at something, thinking about it, and deciding how it works!"

Mr. Poople aims to educate. In past shows, he has explained the color Green and the Difference Between an Arm and a Tail to the adorable regular cast member little Jen Eric, and all the little boys and girls in TV-land. He's helped in his mission by others of his silly yet endearing cast, including wacky Three-Heel Charlie, hug-hungry Teddy, overly optimistic Fat Randy, and the Goofy Woopus.

Unfortunately, there have been some charges that Mr. Poople's show is actually harmful disinformation, not useful education. Some claim that he is just a crazy monkey who thinks his TV show is happening all the time. No one questions Mr. Poople's sincerity, but his "discoveries" are perhaps not as wise or true as he thinks. Take, for instance, his show about the dangers of water and the drying benefits of fire. Although his advice has yet to send anyone to the burn ward, it's only a matter of time. Sock monkey children who can't tell you what state they live in can easily recite the "If you should happen to get wet— find some fire! That's your best bet!" song. There has also been talk that Teddy has been a little indiscriminate with his hugging.

On today's show, Mr. Poople, Teddy, and Three-Heel Charlie explain Nature's wonders to Jen Eric. Here they are, singing a song of Mr. Poople's own composition, "Ev'ry Animal Lays an Egg."

Ev'ry animal lays an egg!
Lays an egg!
Lays an egg!
Be they little or be they big,
ev'ry animal lays an egg!
Ev'ry animal lays an egg!
Lays an egg!
Lays an egg!
Might be ducky or might be pig,
ev'ry animal lays an egg!

MONKEY GOTHIC

It had been a very hard winter for the Kitchen Monkeys. Farmer John's pumpkin crop had not done as well as expected, and Ma was so disgusted that she hit him in the head with her frying pan. This was not unusual, except that the frying pan was still hot. So not only did Farmer John get contuded, but his hat burned up and no one knew where the money for a new one would come from. Savana Banana's "little helper" had wandered off into the snow in search of fresh thread and had not yet returned. It was probably just as well—the green-eyed Monster Monkey was little more than a minibaby mentally, and she usually squooshled the life out of her little helpers after a couple of munce. As soon as the winter passed, someone would have to sneak into the Cracker Barrel to get her a new one. Aunt Lovey's coffeemaker broke, so she was depressed. Even her pink pom-poms looked droopy and tired. Mrs. Tiffany was in the cooking wine, as usual, but all agreed it was worse this year than most. And whenever anyone asked Mama Roux what was in store for the future, Mama just shook her head and said, "Chile, you don't want to know."

Despite it all, the Kitchen Monkeys decided to celebrate with the annual winter feast. With Farmer John in the hospital for his concussion and Cookie and Hummingbird busy with their new-fangled enterprise, the remaining monkeys gathered as much scratch as they could find for a decent meal. As they sat at a table with not quite enough rolls to go around, watching Mrs. Tiffany unsteadily carving the capon, everyone agreed that they were just happy to be together, and that they had more blessings than there were peas in that bowl.

God bless the sock monkey. They endure.

DID YoU KNOW???

Most monkeys work just to have something to do, but Kitchen Monkeys insist on getting tips.

RED GANG VOWS TO INCREASE LURKING, GET 'EM!

(An excerpt from *The Monkey Ape Vine,* Volume 6, Issue 1)

Many citizens are wondering, Is the south side of the Red Heel safe? The narrow walkway bordering the fence next door has been taken over by the Red Gang, who menace arriving innocents with the terrifying cry "Get 'em, Red Gang!" Do they represent a threat to our Old World monkeys and Minibabies?

The Monkey Ape Vine bravely traveled to the south side to find out exactly what motivates this strange new gang of juvenile dollinquents.

Ex-child star Baby Jane seems to be the leader. Since her film career hit the skids, her behavior has become erratic. It's hard to tell if she's actually fronting the Red Gang or if she just thinks she's in a movie. "We're gonna get you and you better look out!" yelled Baby Jane when we interviewed her, then she pointed at the camera and shook her fist. "We're the Red Gang and we're gonna beat every last puppet on the whole grandmom street!" Then she paused and asked, "How was that?"

Her companions, Caesar Goodameche, Kris Krumple, and the Player, looked on impassively. Goodameche, a "made monkey," exhibits definite antisocial tendencies. No one has ever heard him utter a sentence that didn't start with "I don't like." Kris Krumple used to work at Santa Monkey Land, but when that roadside attraction closed, he drifted to the Red Heel. The Player is an ex-spokesman for an athletic shoe company, Mike. It folded because no one realized the obvious: Most sock monkeys don't have feet.

Is the Red Heel's lack of police force or any law enforcement agency responsible for the relative reign of terror enjoyed by the Red Gang? If so, some prominent shelter citizens would rather have the Red Gang than the boys in blue.

"So the Red Gang yell 'Get 'em!' a lot," mused Emily, the Number One Monkey. "Have you ever seen them actually 'get' anybody? Other than painting a bunch of dumb stuff on the side of the Red Heel, what have you ever done to warrant a judge and a cop and all sorts of government? You start down that branch and pretty soon we'll need a constitution. And who'll draft that? Oh yeah. I forgot. *You* will. Reformer." She pointed at me, kind of like Baby Jane had. I don't know who made me more nervous.

"Sure, if they were stealing from GB's Crazy Stuff Store . . . actually, I wouldn't care if they stole from GB's," Emily continued. "If they . . . no, I wouldn't mind that, either. Look, as long as the Red Gang doesn't get in the bed, I figure it can do whatever it wants."

When I told Baby Jane about Emily's comments, she became very upset. "That Emily better know that we mean business and that we are gonna *get her*! And her little bed, too!" Then she turned and started talking to an imaginary director about her motivation.

The Monkey Ape Vine will keep its listeners informed of the situation and let you know if it escalates into an actual threat or simmers at the level of mild annoyance.

REMEMBERING SANTA MONKEY LAND

The Christmas monkey. A surprising number of sock monkeys seem to have been born to celebrate this one time of year, and none epitomize this calling more than the legendary Santa Monkey. He's retired now, but once upon a time, Santa Monkey was the star and the operator of one of the most legendary sock monkey roadside attractions the South has ever seen: Santa Monkey Land!

Housed in a deserted drive-in restaurant just a few miles off Interstate 40, Santa Monkey Land was a dream come true for little sock monkeys who just couldn't wait for Christmastime to come around again. Open year-round, the jingling of bells never stopped. Those days are gone now, but fond memories still linger. Barney and Willajean still talk about that one time they went, when they got married at Pigeon Forge. And it just wasn't a George family Christmas without a visit to Santa Monkey Land.

Layers and layers of Styrofoam shavings covered everything, giving the visitor a lasting souvenir—you got to track a little bit of Santa Monkey Land with you wherever you went! Elves and snowmen frolicked in the foam drifts. Amid the artificial Christmas trees and absurdly giant plastic candy canes raced a quintet of caroling minis from Restorationia called the Five Guys Named Moe. The Moes drove a secretly motorized sleigh pulled by some really cheap-looking fake reindeer ("On Janky! On Hinky!"). When they spied a visitor, they'd steer the sleigh in that direction and throw a brightly colored present—hard.

But the star of the show was always Santa Monkey himself. Strolling from lighted candy cane to rotating oversize cupcake, covered in jingling bells, exuding holidazzle, he was instantly loved by all the little boy and girl monkeys who saw him.

When Santa Monkey Land finally closed—due to Santa Monkey's worsening monkey maladies (walking around in that pretend snow all day made the tips of his toes shrink, and it became impossible for him to walk)—a number of monkeys in the holiday service market were put out of work. Some ended up at the Red Heel. Reindog, the Christmas dog/deer, found work rescuing lost Rounder Monkeys. But poor Kris Krumple fell in with a bad crowd. Krumple drew caricatures of tourists for tips. Now he paints graffiti and hangs with the Red Gang.

For Santa Monkey, retirement at the Red Heel is fine, but he would gladly return to Santa Monkey Land to bring holiday cheer to the Julys of all the good monkey boys and girls on the wrong turnoff. Sometimes he thinks of going back despite his aching feet. But, alas, they tore it down to expand the highway.

PRAISE THE GREAT GRANDMA!

(Transcript from a recent meeting of Brother Rich's Traveling Tent Revival. Featuring the wisdom of sermonator Brother Rich. Mrs. Tiffany, soloist, spreads the Good News through song. Free rubber snakes for the kiddies!)

Friends, I am here to-day to tell you of the Great Grandma! We must take the time and say unto her "Thank you!," for she has been present at all of our births and shall be there on the day we return to the great thread of being.

You may ask, is she watching over us? Is she sitting on her great day-ven-port in the sky seeing that we are made right, and once made, treated right? My friends, I say *no!* She is in the very world around us!

Now, friends, I know this shall come to you as a shock, but tonight I say unto you: We are made by our people cousins! We did not spring forth from the great factory in the eastern sky, nor were we made from whole cloth!

No, do not chatter amongst yourselves to shut out this knowledge, for it is true. And this is Good News! For it is in the spirit of the Great Grandma that we are created! She entereth into the hands of every one of our people cousins who seweth monkey with stitches and sock! She guideth the maker with her hand, begetting a new creation from the humblest of materials! Our designer is intelligent and so is our design!

And the Great Grandma never leaves us! No, friends! Not when our eyes are sewn on, not when our last seam is shut, and not when we are dressed. For who knoweth when life truly begins for the sock monkey? Only Grandma, from whose crafty hands we all springeth!

And whenever we groweth old, and are covered with rends all over our body from this veil of tears, she is still with us and can take us up, brethren! And as she sews, so shall she repair! So I say unto you tonight, don't fear the repair! Don't fear the repair, for it is guided by the Great Grandma, and by the repair, so can you be sewn again!

Friends, we have so many reasons to be thankful to the Great Grandma! She has seen fit to give us arms, tails, and sometimes noses! And she has ensured that each of us is an individual, none exactly like another! I myself have been blessed with my hat, and my overalls, and I have a pair of black felt boots that Great Grandma ordained unto my feet at birth! But mostly I am thankful I was made, so I can be with you today, to share her good word!

Needle to needle, thread to thread! AMEN!

DID YOU KNOW???

"Grandma!" is the worst swear word in sock monkey language. It's even worse than calling somebody a "puppet." Taking your creator's name in vain is always bad news.

as She sews,
so shall
She repair...

ROOM 1009: THE ELECTRIC KOOL-AID ACID WASH

For years, JoJo belonged to Crazy Eye, but Crazy Eye didn't know it. Crazy Eye owned a second-hand clothing store. She bought all the old clothes she could find and even had to rent a warehouse for all her garbage bags of old clothes. The bags were stacked from floor to ceiling. In one of these bags, near the bottom, was JoJo. JoJo lived in this bag until his whole world became nothing but the clothes he was lying in. No light, no air, nobody. Just clothes.

Eventually, Crazy Eye excavated the bag and found JoJo in it. She couldn't even remember seeing him before. She had heard about the Red Heel Monkey Shelter, so she sent him there to live.

Dazed by the light, almost squooshled flat by the weight of the clothes, JoJo had trouble adjusting to a world that wasn't all material. When he arrived at the shelter, JoJo made for the first pile of clothes he saw.

Soon, JoJo began hanging around laundry baskets. JoJo never bothers with the dirty clothes. He likes them clean, and the fresher from the dryer the better. Whenever he isn't amid clothes, he twitches and writhes and runs nervously in place. JoJo is a basket case. His ability to socialize has been severely hampered by his obsession. JoJo is a clothes addict, a monkey on his own back.

All JoJo ever talks about is clothes. On days when the laundry is put away and nothing is available from the dryer, JoJo sits in a corner, mumbling. "Man, I wish I had some whites right now. Whites are the best. Thin fresh T-shirts and underwear . . . and socks, man. Burrow down in a fluffy mound of tube socks and just fly. Whites, man. They're like clouds. And jeans. I could float away on a sea of jeans. Darks and browns are so earthy, and reds and pinks are fiery and intense. They're cool, but if I had my druthers, I'd take a basket of whites."

Research indicates that JoJo's case is extremely rare. Clothing addiction seems to arise from a prolonged and isolated exposure to clothes. Casual contact is neither habit forming, nor mood altering. Still, it would perhaps be wise to say no to clothes.

DID YOU KNOW???

Monkey maladies and addictions are not the end of the world. Question Monk suffers from a huge hernia, Samantha Brown has mouth bleed, and, as you may have heard, Happy George has more back holes than whole back.

HERE LIES
GIVEAWAY

BETTER TO
BURN THAN
FADE AWAY

SOCK MONKEY SEMATARY

Sock monkey dreams are not always made of sugarplums. There are those who believe that strange things reside in the cobwebby, dank basement below the monkey shelter. Behind a door most would prefer remained closed, accessible only by a series of rickety stairs through which one might fall during any point of descent, lies the Red Hell.

Late at night, the legions of the darned creep outside to howl and cavort beneath the pale moon. There is no comfort, no warmth, in these creatures—to hug them would only prove clammy and goose-graving.

But just who is haunting Heel House?

Rumors circulate of Frick and Frack, twin monkey-snakes whose devious whispers, angering lies, and tempting promises are difficult to disbelieve, let alone resist. Igor Yetch has been seen henching his way through the Red Halls late at night, searching for some master for whom he might do evil bidding. And it is said that Ed the Head, though disembodied, can still speak, see, hear, and, perhaps most distressingly, bounce.

Yet all these night creatures are only a nuisance compared to the malignant and merciless middlemost Monster Monkey—the hoobajoob. Drawn to any location where more than five sock monkeys have gathered, the hoobajoob lies in wait, beneath couches and beds, behind bookcases and in little-used pantryways, just out of sight, waiting for an incautious or unfortunate sock monkey to fall on the floor. Once the hoobajoob spies a victim, it scurries from its hiding place,

leaps, and cuts its prey to pieces with its rusty scissors, in a screaming, giddy violence of threads and shreds.

Who can hold back this dark night of the sole? Thankfully, there is the mysterious Spooky, who floats through the night with no fear of the supernatural. What is Spooky? Is he a ghost, his body lost to the flashing blades of a hoobajoob? Or was he sewn with the gossamer socks of some unknown spirit? Either way, Spooky has seen many a Rounder Monkey home through the cold, pale moonlight when others wanted to rend the unwary traveler seam from seam.

Tonight Spooky is watching over the grave of Giveaway, a onetime resident of the Red Heel, who was immolated in a tragic barbecue accident one October night. There are those that say Frick and Frack slithered up behind him in his last moments, whispering, "Sssparks! Sssparks are pretty! You could catch one and take it to a ffffine maiden . . . Mofffie, or sssweet Sssamantha Brown. You could catch one, Giveaway! They are prettier than ffflowersss. What a fine gift, a ssscinder. Go on. There isss a ssstray! Reach for it!"

Polyfill and cotton batting go up like dry kindling. No one could do anything to save him.

Comes the dawn, when the light of the day begins to subtly brighten the Appalachian mountainscape, the gibbering gibbon ghouls vanish from the hillside, their revels at an end. And in the musty, moist basement of the Red Heel, spiderwebs remain unbroomed, dust settles on soft and hard object alike, and whatever waits there, waits alone.

HERE LIES
GIVEAWAY
BETTER TO
BURN THAN
FADE AWAY

THE IMPULSE TO ART

Jacobean Stock, the artist, was throwing a fit. His latest exhibit at the Peanut Gallery was well attended (although he would have enjoyed a larger audience had he included "Free rubber snakes for the kiddies" as a tagline on his flyer), but his paintings were receiving baffled stares, dismissive headshakes, and infuriating questions from observers, the most offensive of which was, "Who arted?" Finally, he swung a spare brush from his satchel and chased everyone from the gallery, threatening to permanently stain them or at the very least send them to the cleaners.

"Never again!" he fumed, pacing anxiously. "If I have to hear one more monkey ask me, 'Is that a person or is that a bear?,' I shall tear the ears from my head, else stitch them shut!! And it is a *landscape*! Neither bear nor man! Oh, the common folk know nothing of art! I must quit this place."

Jacobean Stock decided then and there he would retreat to the Red Shed, a dilapidated building behind the Red Heel, to live a life of austere contemplation and painting. This would have been fine with everyone, but Jacobean had to make an artistic exit. "I am taking leave of you, dollies! I leave you silly jackanapes to your games, japes, and incessant chatter! I hope you enjoy your foolish folkish foofoorah! I shall be out back, creating, should anyone decide to join me on a higher plane."

This outburst caught the attention of Pierre Mon Frère, the Red Heel's major Mischief Monkey.

"Oh! Hey! Jake-O B-S! 'Oo do vouz think vouz is?" yelled Pierre. But the artist was already out of earshot.

"Excusez my French, but, 'ow you say, 'Fooly folking foofie rah?' Zee bloostering ponce is thinking zee high arts is more clevair than us folk arts, non? Pierre will defend zee honair of zee Red Heel! Pierre will show high art who is bettair! He will challenge zat paintair to . . . zee duwell!"

Meanwhile, in the Red Shed, Jacobean Stock's work was not going well. "Any chimpanzee with a paintbrush could do what I am doing!" he wailed in despair. "I am blocked! My work is flat . . . two-dimensional . . . self-conscious! But I must press on! I must break through!" He went back to his work.

Up in the rafters, Pierre Mon Frère carefully crept along a crossbeam until he was right above his target. He quietly scootched a paint can directly over Jacobean's latest work. "Now I will show how zee primitive technique and natural buckét stroke can ovaircome years of training with one push of zee bottóm! Daa-daa!" He tipped the can over.

Accustomed to quick getaways, Pierre was off the rafters and out the window while the screams of shock were still echoing like a chorus through the Red Shed. These screams were like music to Pierre's ears, but if he had stuck around, he would have heard a different tune.

"The effect . . . Yes! So spontaneous! So evocative! So vibrant and expressive! This is wonderful! It completely cures my block! Random-rafter-canvas-splatting is my wave of the future! Bless you, my angel of the paint can, whoever you were! Truly, you are from a higher plane!"

THE LEGACY OF THE GEORGE FAMILY

CAPPY   OLLIE   PAPPY   MAMMY   HAPPY   GINNIE   SPARKY

The Georges are a distinguished family of sock monkeys preeminent in the fields of entertainment and *Sockosimian* social progress. Almost no major moment in monkey history has happened without the presence of a George. Spread out across the country and into every major level of society, the Georges' influence and renown casts a shadow no other monkey family can match.

Cappy George came to prominence by inventing the pomerator, making mass pom-pom production possible. Once worn by only the most affluent, pom-poms became the standard accessory worn around the neck and arms during the sock monkey population explosion, thanks to Cappy's invention. Strangely enough, Georges themselves rarely affect pom-poms.

Ollie George achieved worldwide fame as the ringmaster of the GAGA OSME Circus. Pappy George took up Cappy's legacy. After Sockton Sinclair's controversial book *In the Pom-pom Jungle* was published, Pappy became an advocate for pom-pom factory reform. He kept the best of Cappy's industrial innovations while making sure working conditions were as safe and sane as possible. As Pappy's wife, Mammy George wielded her influence in the service of monkey education. She also raised Happy, Ginnie, and Sparky as fitting heirs to the George name.

Not all famous Georges live at the Red Heel. Another prominent George is Brainy, scientist and inventor of the theory of relatives. He resides in a northeastern sock monkey warren. His portrait graced the cover of another recent book-length study.

Georges are not necessarily made by the same monkey maker. How a George comes into the world is not known, but the regularity of their appearance and profligacy of their population is sometimes cited as reason to believe in the Great Grandma.

In addition to their inherent dignity and almost mystical aura of destiny, George monkeys have many distinct physical characteristics. Widely spaced dark button eyes, touching and slightly overlapping the snout; round, hatless heads (Georges rarely wear the traditional monkey hat, although as we can see they are not above fezzes, bonnets, and driver's caps); "up" mouths (usually unlined); no nostrils; and protruding ears. There are variations, of course, but study the Georges in this photo, and the family traits should become evident.

Anyone who thinks they know of the presence of more members of the George family should contact *The Monkey Ape Vine,* so we can continue to reunite this great sock monkey family with other members of their clan. The Georges that live at the Red Heel are sick of seeing just one another at the annual George family reunion and are looking forward to meeting and reuniting with other Georges.

YEE-HAW
INDUSTRIES

WHAT DO YOU GOT
THAT I CAN TAKE?

2 Month
FREE

rock monkey makings

PLASTIC FANG

TIRE
.... comes
with tire
flattener

SUNDAY MAY 2

GB's
DELLA BAR

GAGA OSAKE

no
sale

NO
COMMITMENT

CRAZY STUFF STORE

GB'S CRAZY STUFF STORE

Come one! Come down! Come in! To GB's Crazy Stuff Store! GB gots more last-hand goods than you can shake stick at! And if you shake stick at GB's goods, you better not knock them over, because if you break 'em you buy 'em!

GB'S CRAZY STUFF STORE filled to ceiling with most fabulous stuff monkeys could ever want to need! Culled from the finest boxes of trash and garbage all over Red Heel Monkey Shelter, GB's inventory is constantly growing! We bring in more stuff than goes out the door so you, GB's customer, can have pick of litter!

GB's Crazy Stuff Store! Home of famous Baboon Mask! Home of GB's dolla bin! Home of famous monkey spoon, old blue frog, and the mysterious Monkey Pawn! Find "I saw Monkey Pawn" Post-its for sale in GB's Crazy Stuff Store souvenir gift shop!

Just in! Mushroom decoy! Mushroom hunting much better with mushroom decoy! Fool mushrooms into thinking it's safe to grow near mushroom decoy, then pick them off! Just in! Genie lamp! Genie not included. Back in stock! All ear earrings! Get in on latest fashion trend! Available in yellow, black, and red! Got sporks? We got sporks!

Check out tire flattener! Tire flattener very practical item and very easy to use when you need flat tire! Step one: Get tire! (GB cuts out middleman—tire flattener comes with tire!) Step two: Insert metal end into tire! Step three: Tire goes flat! It's just that easy! Ask Reggie and Loretta, former owners of tire flattener! They will tell you! Flattens tires flat!

Got stuff you don't need? Stuff you're not using? Stuff you don't want? Stuff you don't remember? Bring it into GB's! GB will take it! What do you got that I can take? GB does not work on consignment or give cash, but GB will trade your stuff for GB's stuff as long as your stuff is better! Otherwise, GB will just take it!

Not in the area? Check out GB-Bay, GB's latest marketing innovation! Many fabulous items on sale at GB-Bay, but you must come to showroom for most exclusive latest stuff! GB's business is expanding like crazy! GB take in almost six pieces of money yesterday! New store record!

Naysayers say GB's store is wrong! Say that sock monkeys not cut out to be in business! Say sock monkeys are out of date and overrated. Say sock monkeys can't compete in modern world! GB says naysayers are wrong!

WHY? BECAUSE GB IS CRAZY! THAT'S WHY!

WE WERE HERE FIRST!
BY STELLA AND JUNE

Hello! We are Stella and June! We are twin monkeys who sit on our shelf in Loretta's room, with our kitty and our pictures. We were very mad at Benny Hathaway for a long time, because he shooshed us and sent us away when we tried to give him some news about Emily, who is always going around saying she is the Number One Monkey!

But now Benny Hathaway has said that we can have a minute to speak! So now we are less mad at Benny than we were, although we still don't like being shooshed! But at least we are going to get to say what we have to say!

What we have to say is this: Emily is *not* the Number One Monkey! *We* are the Number One Monkey!

And we can prove it!

We were Loretta's monkeys from when she was a Little Girl. She carried us around with her and told us stories.

One day, Loretta's mom put us into a box full of Loretta's other things. She gave these boxes to Loretta but did not tell her what was in them. Loretta was very busy and just moved the boxes around with her wherever she went, knowing that someday she would open them.

We sat in that box for munce and munce. We were waiting patiently for Loretta to open it and let us out again! But Loretta didn't know we were in the box. When she and Reggie started looking for sock monkeys, they talked about their first monkeys, and Loretta told Reggie about us. But she said she did not know where we were. She did not realize we were in the attic right above them!

The next time Reggie and Loretta moved, Loretta decided she was finally going to go through all of her old boxes and see what was in them. She opened our box, and there we were! She was so happy to see us, she grabbed us and hugged us and said, "I'm sorry! I'm sorry! I'm sorry!"

We didn't know why she was sorry, because we were not mad at Loretta, but when we came up from the basement (because we were in the basement and not the attic this time), we could not believe how many monkeys had come to live with her! Reggie was bad enough, but the other monkeys were ridiculous!

Worst of all was Emily, because she was so stuffed full of herself, calling herself the Number One Monkey! She was not the Number One Monkey, though. We were at the very first Red Heel before Emily was there, only nobody knew it. And we were the reason why Loretta liked monkeys to begin with. Without us, she probably never would have gotten Emily!

So Emily didn't start the shelter! We started the shelter! And we never get any credit!

LAST THOUGHTS WITH VAN DYKE BREEZE

My name is Van Dyke Breeze. I write a zine called *Ticket Stubs.* It's the Red Heel Monkey Shelter's alternative media outlet. It's mostly a music zine—I write about records and shows and stuff. The Red Heel is pretty vibrant musically. Everybody seems to sing, even if they can't. Sometimes I put in news Benny Hathaway misses.

When I found out Benny was going to publish a book on the RHMS, I was worried. *The Monkey Ape Vine* is pretty good for a mainstream paper, but I thought he would have to compromise our structural integrity to present us to peoples. I planned to do an exposé on some of the book's inaccuracies after it came out, just to get the truth out there.

Mostly, I was mad because I wasn't in any of the pictures.

But then Benny Hathaway asked me to write the afterword to the book and really showed me a lot of respect, which I thought was really great considering that he is a published author and I am just a guy who handwrites a zine and puts it out on old fax paper.

Still, I do think Benny got some things wrong. The whole "Emily Is Number One" thing is very controversial. Happy George's show was totally classic when it was *Happy in the Morning,* but he lost his edge when he moved to nights. Question Monk's earliest recordings may be the pinnacles of primate pound-screech,

but after he hired BoJangle Duke as his manager he went down the tubes artistically. The Cool Girls are actually kind of snooty, and Rabéla always beats me to the new stuff in GB's dolla bin. Brian Wilson did *not* own Mrs. Tiffany. Monkey High-Rise is really just a bookshelf. The Who Wants to Marry Mollie contest was fixed. Barney's bow tie is a clip-on. Orlo is not made out of socks. It's called Punch Buggy, not Slug Bug. The Windmere Treatment kind of hurts.

Otherwise, I think that Benny Hathaway did a good job of documenting the scene, and I can give this book a good review. I guess it was pretty tough to do, to take something that was in all of our heads and make it so you could read and see it. So, thanks, Benny.

Good hunting!

VAN DYKE BREEZE

Hmmm . . . Maybe it wasn't the smartest idea I ever had to give the last word to those guys.

I guess that that's it, peoples. I, for one, have mixed emotions now that we're at the end of the book. I was reading through Jorge Luis Borges's *Book of Imaginary Beings,* and I came across this passage: "Descartes tells us that monkeys could speak if they wished to, but they prefer to keep silent so they won't be made to work." Sometimes through the munce it's taken to put this project together, I've wondered if I shouldn't have kept my big mouth sewn shut. But now that it's over, I know it's been worth it. Thanks for taking the time to stop in at the Red Heel Monkey Shelter. I hope you've enjoyed your stay.

Benny Hathaway

SOCK MONKEY DREAMS

Daily Life at the Red Heel Monkey Shelter

WRITTEN AND CREATED BY
WHITNEY SHROYER
AND LETITIA WALKER

PHOTOGRAPHY
BY MICHAEL TRAISTER

DIORAMAS CONSTRUCTED BY MICHAEL TRAISTER AND LETITIA WALKER

ACKNOWLEDGMENTS

This project never could have been completed without an almost endless list of friends, family, well-wishers, and supporters. The folks below found monkeys, made monkeys, helped with props and sets or offered connections and inspiration. If it takes a village to raise a child, it takes a whole city to run a shelter. We would especially like to thank those on the list who are putting up with us making monkeys out of them. If anyone feels left out, blame Pierre Mon Frère, because he totally swiped your name from the list.

The photograph of the Red Heel Monkey Shelter is actually A Bed of Roses, a Victorian bed-and-breakfast hotel, in Asheville, North Carolina. Thanks, Janis Ortwein!

Cathy Fowler
Meg Leder and Rebecca Behan
Christine DiBenedetto and the Rebelles
Rebecca and Evar Hecht
Simon, Christi, and Vivian Whiteley
Eldorado Salvage and Mid-Century Modern
Alisa Carswell
Cat Kerr
Katie Crawford and Scott Kinnebrew
Gnomi Baloney
Linda Hamlin (the Lady in Pink)
Lucius Monkey, Iggy and the Langs
Olivia, Brian, and Fluff TV/Super Happy Fun Land
Dennis Jones and MixMonk
Joy Pascarella and Lacie Beh
Annie and Supermonk
Melanie Johnson-Moxley and the Sunnyflower Farm
The Red Heel Message Boarders
Rich Smith and Kathi Frey
Ilene Van Abbema

Rebeccah Mark and Minx
Debbie Goard
Dana Gooden
John Powers and Nicole Kintz
Sara Legatski
G. Craig Hobbs
Greg, Esther, and Ruby
Jeff Breeze
Kevin Bradley and Julie Belcher of Yee Haw Industries
Bob Downing
Randi Coddington
Kathy Rawdon
Janelle Hessig
Lynn Williams
Karen and Orlo Shroyer
Jim and Jan Walker
Anne Russell
Gail and Virginia Purdy
Koni Purdy
Ron and Kristi Carper
Joyce Holt
Rebekah, David, and Iris Richards

TOP TEN

SLEAZY HUGH PICKUP LINES

10. Nice pair.
9. Wanna come upstairs and take a look at my stitchings?
8. What's a girl like you doing on a shelf like this?
7. Wanna guess my password?
6. Your pom-poms are exquisite. They add considerably to your beauty. They look quite soft.
5. You know how to whistle, don't you? Well, I don't, either.
4. Put me on your guest list, baby!
3. It'll be artistic.
2. Have you hugged your Hugh today?
1. Is that your tail between your legs or are you just happy to see me?

Chris Bower
Fred and Melody Traister
Patricia Traister
Stacey Traister
A. Doran
Adam Strange
Gabe Viles
Chris Benedict
Jeremiah and Jessie Kidwell
Mark Walters
John Schooley
Kenton Robertson
Ronnie Tomany
Mr. Mouse
Serenity Eyre
Congo
Opal and Orson
The teddy bears of Henry Hager and Adele Hager Saunders
Chad McRorie
Rob Castillo
Terri Adams
Jimmy McMillan
Jill Tieman and Mira
David Zabriskie
Susie Millions
Rick Melby
Anitta Charleson
Western Lanes, Raleigh, North Carolina
North Carolina Fairground Flea Market
Lon Murdick
Rob Ovitt and Jenée Navlin at Izzy's Coffee Den
Lisa Shoemaker and Make Me Fabric
Father and Son Antiques
Lexington Park Antiques
The Apple Wagon
The Screen Door
Chatsworth Antiques
Kelly Gold

Smiley's Flea Market
Habitat for Humanity
Sean Moser
Gabby
Tori
Red Lips/Red Ass
Claire Ashby
Wootini
Carrie Harder
Pullen Memorial Baptist Church
Steve McBride
Bill Griffith
Lark Books
Steve Mace
Coco, Ginger, and Cinnamon
Little Pauline and The Depot in Biltmore Village
Dani Moffie
Travis Medford

And all of the unknown monkey makers who made so many of these monkeys, blessing them with so much personality and spirit. The Great Grandma surely worked through your hands.